The Quiet Hustle

Balancing Stress with Stillness

Wes Bozarth

The Quiet Hustle: Balancing Stress with Stillness

ISBN: 979-8-9918440-1-7

Published by Wes Bozarth

Owensboro, Kentucky

This is a work of nonfiction. While the author has made every effort to ensure that the information in this book is accurate, it is not intended as a substitute for professional advice. The author disclaims any liability in connection with the use of the information presented.

Cover design by Wes & Amanda Bozarth

Printed in the United States of America

First Edition: October 2024

For those seeking calm in the chaos,

may you find your path here.

Contents

Preface

Life works in poetic ways, don't you think? We often try to find meaning in separate events, linking them to coincidence, fate, or even divine intervention. While some things are impossible to prove, I choose to believe there's beauty in the symmetry of life. Looking back now, I realize that my journey toward balancing success with peace was a line in my life's poem that I never expected, but one that changed everything.

I've always enjoyed the time I spent in the world between my two ears, even if that world wasn't always calm. As a child, I rehearsed countless scenarios, anticipating every possible outcome to avoid life's pitfalls. This habit stayed with me, and it wasn't long before it became a way to cope with the uncertainties of life. I became the master of overthinking, of always planning, always anticipating, always preparing for that next "what if."

As I grew older, my tendency to live in my head didn't fade—it only intensified. Instead of focusing on what truly mattered, I became consumed with the day-to-day anxieties: *What's next? Why am I not in a leadership role yet? Am I doing enough to stand out? Should I stay late at work to show my dedication?* The need to stay ahead, be perfect, and anticipate every possible failure became a relentless cycle that I thought was the path to success.

You might be thinking, "Wes, you need to calm down," and you'd be right. I needed to calm down, but back then, I believed that this way of thinking was my edge. It wasn't until life, in its poetic way, forced me to confront my own unsustainable pace that I began to understand how wrong I'd been.

Halloween Horror

It was Halloween night in 2020, a year most of us would love to forget. My wife, brother, sister-in-law, and I attended a Halloween party hosted by my lifelong friend, Landon. As a tribute to the popular show Yellowstone, my wife and I dressed as Beth and Rip. There was something about embodying Rip—the simple, immovable cowboy— that made me feel especially confident that night.

Landon and I have always been competitive, and it wasn't long before our friendly rivalry flared up again. This time, it took the form of an arm-wrestling match. With the whole party gathered around, we cleared the table and locked hands, ready to prove ourselves once more. As the countdown began, I felt sure of my strength, sure of my ability to win against my friend. But then, in a heartbeat, everything changed.

A sharp crack echoed through the room, as if a gunshot had gone off. Pain surged through my arm, and I realized with horror that my humerus had shattered. Landon immediately jumped back, his hands on his face like a kid caught in a prank gone wrong. I sat there, my right arm sagging, tingling, and radiating pain. In that moment, I was no longer the self-assured cowboy—I was just a man brought to his knees by his own stubborn need to win.

The Aftermath and the Spiral

The arm-wrestling injury should have been a warning—a clear sign that my relentless pursuit of success at all costs was unsustainable. At the time, I was a newly hired Quality Engineer/Continuous Improvement Coordinator, living in Owensboro, Kentucky, and commuting over an hour each way to Bowling Green for work. Fortunately, I was allowed to work from home as my arm healed, and what should have felt like a relief soon became a breeding ground for my anxieties.

I began questioning everything: Was my boss questioning my productivity? Did my colleagues think I wasn't contributing enough? Was my career at risk because I wasn't physically present? I tried to prove my worth by working harder, pushing myself to the point of exhaustion, and letting my mind spiral into the same old, destructive pattern. Every email, every ping, every moment of silence, *everything* became a reason to worry, a sign that I wasn't doing enough.

In March 2021, things took another turn. My wife and I bought a new home, and shortly afterward, I started experiencing severe gastrointestinal distress. I lost over 30 pounds in two months and spent countless hours visiting doctors and searching the web, trying to find answers. When I was eventually diagnosed with Lymphocytic Colitis, I realized that my body was reacting to the very stress and anxiety that had consumed my mind for so long. It was a harsh wake-up call, but it was also the turning point I needed.

New Friends, New Habits, New Practice

It wasn't until we moved into our new home that things began to change. Our neighborhood was more than I could have hoped for—a close-knit group of friends from all walks of life who genuinely cared for one another. They taught me the value of living in the present, of finding joy in the small moments, and of constantly learning from those around you.

One of the most impactful lessons I've learned is a simple truth shared by Bill Nye, yes, THE Science Guy (childhood hero): "Everyone you'll ever meet knows something you don't." I've been fortunate to be surrounded by remarkable people who have enriched my life with their knowledge and perspectives. Whether from family and friends, instructors and mentors, or even authors and podcasters, I've been inspired by a constant curiosity and the drive to learn. I'm deeply grateful for the wisdom they've imparted, and for the ability to absorb and apply these lessons throughout my journey.

The Road to Balance

In November 2021, months after my arm had healed and I returned to work, I transitioned to a new position that no longer tied me to a single site, but required me to support multiple production sites. While this change was welcome—being based out of my home and no more daily two-and-a-half-hour drives—my old neurotic tendencies again crept back in. I found myself stuck in my head, preparing for situations that may or may not happen, overly concerned with making sure I was having an impact.

This new role required a fair amount of travel, which I was comfortable with. Anyone who knows me can attest that I'm fine with solitude—perhaps *too* comfortable. Even when being in my own head isn't helping me, I can easily retreat there, where I have little need for external stimulus. After a few months of traveling from site to site, I acclimated to this new pace, and while I felt like I was doing meaningful work that was being recognized, I still couldn't shake the feeling that I was 'hustling' too hard just to have an impact. I knew there had to be a more sustainable way to live successfully. This realization fueled my passion for researching how to work more productively, build relationships, and maintain inner peace.

I'm grateful for the time I've spent on the road. Don't get me wrong, I miss my wife, family, and friends when I'm away, but I've used this time to practice perseverance and commit to learning how to live a balanced life—one where I can achieve success without sacrificing my peace.

This book explores these ideas in detail, but it's important to touch on them here: as you proceed down this path you *will* have to make difficult decisions—you'll have to choose to go home and rest instead of staying out another hour with friends. You'll have to dedicate some evenings to that passion project that needs your attention. You'll have to carve out time for your own self-care. At first, these things may seem hard but take solace in knowing that as you continue to align your goals with your values, they will get easier, and you'll feel deeply fulfilled by the value-driven life you're creating.

This doesn't mean you place less value on your relationships. In fact, maintaining strong, meaningful connections is a crucial part of living a balanced life. It's important to nurture these relationships in healthy ways, ensuring they contribute to your growth and well-being rather than adding to your stress. True connection comes from the quality of the time you spend together, not the quantity. Learning to set boundaries doesn't mean distancing yourself from loved ones—it means being present and fully engaged when you are with them, rather than feeling stretched too thin.

At the same time, you may find that certain relationships no longer serve your peace. This can be one of the hardest lessons to learn: letting go of relationships that drain your energy or pull you away from your values. It's not about cutting people off; but recognizing when a relationship has become imbalanced or unhealthy. It's about creating space for those who support your journey and respect the boundaries you set to maintain your inner peace. Letting go can be painful, but it often leads to deeper fulfillment, as it opens up room for connections that truly align with your values and the life you're striving to build.

As I spent time on the road in study and contemplation, and began to align my work, relationships, and personal growth with my core values, it became clear that finding balance wasn't just a personal need—it was a universal challenge faced by many. The constant pressure to achieve, the fear of letting others down, and the inner turmoil that accompanies overworking aren't unique to me. This realization is what led me to write this book.

Why I Wrote This Book

If you've ever felt trapped by your own thoughts, constantly chasing an ideal version of success while losing sight of what truly matters, this book is for you. It's for anyone who's been overwhelmed by the pressures of life, who's felt the strain of trying to do more, be more, achieve more. It's a guide for those who, like me, are searching for a way to balance the drive for success with the need for peace.

My hope is that by sharing my story, you'll find encouragement, inspiration, and practical tools to help you on your journey. Life works in poetic ways, and if you're willing to explore it, you might just find that your path to success isn't about striving harder—but about finding a way to thrive with a calm, centered mind.

As you read through this book, remember that my goal is simple: to help improve the lives of anyone who, like me, has struggled to find both success and peace. And if you ever want to share your thoughts, questions, or stories, I'd love to hear from you. Feel free to reach out at wbozarth@live.com.

As I prepare to publish this book on October 31, 2024, exactly four years after that fateful Halloween night, I'm reminded once more that *life truly does work in poetic ways*.

The Quiet Hustle

Balancing Stress with Stillness

Introduction

Redefining Success

In a world where wealth, titles, and accomplishments often measure success, it's easy to fall into a cycle of striving, only to find that each time we reach a goal, the finish line shifts further away. We've been conditioned to believe that success requires sacrifice: our time, health, and, most significantly, peace of mind. But what if the true measure of success wasn't found in external achievements alone? What if the journey toward our goals could be just as fulfilling as the destination? This book explores the idea that lasting success is not an outcome, but a balance—a harmony between ambition and inner peace. This journey doesn't ask you to give up your dreams; instead, it invites you to redefine them to honor your personal aspirations and well-being.

But this idea of balance is far from the norm. We live in a culture that glorifies achievement, where success is too often defined by endless hustle and external validation. From a young age, we are taught to associate our self-worth with what we can accomplish, not who we are. This belief is ingrained in us through various experiences, shaping how we view ourselves and our value in the world:

- **Academic Achievements:** Consider how children are often praised primarily for their grades, awards, or athletic accomplishments. Instead of valuing qualities like kindness, empathy, or curiosity, the focus tends to be on how many A's are on a report card or how many trophies line the shelf. This conveys that our worth is tied to what we can produce or achieve rather than who we are as individuals.[1]

- **Social Media Validation:** In today's digital world, our sense of self-worth can become deeply entangled with the number of likes, comments, or followers we have online. We begin to measure our value by how "successful" our posts are, seeking validation from others rather than appreciating our unique qualities. This constant comparison and desire for approval reinforce the idea that our worth is dependent on external validation.[2]

- **Career Titles and Salaries:** As adults, the tendency to equate our value with our professional roles becomes even more pronounced. Introductions often include job titles—"successful lawyer" or "senior executive"—implying that our careers define our identity and worth. We may begin to feel that without a prestigious job title or a high salary, we somehow fall short.

- **Material Success:** Society frequently measures success by the accumulation of material possessions. Owning the latest gadgets, driving a luxury car, or living in an upscale neighborhood can become markers of self-worth. We start believing that our value increases with every new possession rather than finding fulfillment in who we are and our connections with others.

- **Competitive Sports and Hobbies:** For many, the pressure to excel begins on the playing field. Young athletes often hear praise only when they win, while the effort, teamwork, and love for the game go unnoticed. This reinforces the notion that they are only as good as their latest performance, creating a mindset that their value depends on whether they come out on top.[3]

- **Cultural Expectations:** In some cultures, specific life milestones—such as getting married, having children, or achieving professional success by a certain age—become benchmarks for self-worth. The pressure to meet these expectations can make us feel inadequate if we don't follow the predetermined path, overshadowing our happiness or growth.[4]

These examples illustrate how, from childhood to adulthood, we're often conditioned to tie our self-worth to external achievements and societal expectations. But real success—the kind that nourishes both ambition *and* inner peace—requires redefining how we measure our value. It's about recognizing that our worth is not determined by what we accomplish but by who we are, how we treat others, and the fulfillment we find in our journey.

The relentless pursuit of success—whether it's the next promotion, the perfect life on social media, or financial milestones—feeds into the growing "hustle culture." It tells us that we will feel fulfilled only through constant striving, longer hours, and more accolades. Yet, this pressure to consistently achieve more has a downside that many only recognize once they've reached their goals: the sense of emptiness and burnout that follows.

The Societal Pressure to Succeed

Society celebrates productivity, pushing individuals to achieve at all costs. We are bombarded with images of "successful" people who seem to have it all, further fueling the idea that we need to do more constantly. In this narrative, moments of stillness or self-care are often seen as indulgences, reserved for when all the hard work is finished. But for many, the work never truly ends. Focusing on external achievements alone can lead to an imbalanced life, where burnout and stress replace the satisfaction we thought success would bring.

This relentless pursuit often exhausts us, longing for a peace that seems perpetually out of reach. Studies have shown that chronic stress and overwork can lead to severe mental and physical health issues, ranging from anxiety and depression to heart disease and weakened immune systems. [5] We pay a high price for this constant chase, sacrificing our well-being in the name of an elusive ideal.

Yet, there's an alternative to this frenetic pace—one rooted in the simple act of 'being' rather than always 'doing.' When we allow ourselves moments of stillness, we discover space for reflection, creativity, and genuine connection. In these quiet intervals, we find that life is not solely defined by the items checked off our to-do lists, but by the experiences that bring us joy and fulfillment.

Many cultures recognize the value of balance, emphasizing the importance of rest and mindfulness. For example, the Danish concept of "hygge" celebrates comfort, warmth, and simple pleasures, [6] while Japan's "ikigai" encourages finding purpose in everyday life. [7] These philosophies remind us that happiness and productivity are not mutually exclusive—they can coexist when we make room for both.

Perhaps it's time to redefine what success truly means. Rather than chasing endless achievements, we can focus on cultivating a life that feels rich and meaningful from the inside out. Self-care, far from being a luxury, becomes an essential part of this journey, a way to recharge and reconnect with what genuinely matters. In doing so, we not only protect our well-being, but we also find a more profound sense of satisfaction that no external accolade can provide.

The Consequences: Burnout and Emptiness

Yet, for all the external markers of success, many find themselves feeling empty or unfulfilled once they've reached their goals. This paradox stems from a profound imbalance between external achievements and internal well-being. Burnout, characterized by exhaustion, detachment, and a reduced sense of accomplishment, is now more prevalent than ever in high-achieving cultures. According to a

2019 report by the World Health Organization (WHO), burnout has become such a widespread issue that it was officially recognized as an "occupational phenomenon." The report defines burnout as a syndrome resulting from chronic workplace stress that hasn't been successfully managed, with symptoms including energy depletion, increased mental distance from one's job, and a sense of ineffectiveness. [8]

Recent studies further highlight the alarming rise of burnout across various professions. For instance, a survey conducted by Gallup in 2020 found that 76% of employees experience burnout on the job at least sometimes, and 28% reported feeling burned out "very often" or "always." This high prevalence is particularly notable in high-pressure industries such as healthcare, finance, and technology, where the expectation of being constantly available and productive is ingrained in the culture. [9]

One striking example is the tech industry, where long hours, relentless deadlines, and a culture that glorifies "hustling" often contribute to severe burnout. A survey by Blind, an anonymous workplace community app, revealed that more than 57% of tech employees experienced burnout during the pandemic, with companies like Amazon and Facebook reporting some of the highest rates.[10] This trend suggests that even industries at the forefront of innovation grapple with overwork's detrimental effects.

The consequences of burnout are not limited to individual well-being but also impact organizational performance. Research published in the "Harvard Business Review" found that burned-out employees are

63% more likely to take sick days and have a 13% lower level of confidence in their performance. Moreover, companies with high rates of burnout experience higher turnover rates, reduced productivity, and increased healthcare costs, proving that this issue affects not just individuals but entire organizations. [11]

Real-world examples also shed light on this phenomenon. In 2019, the Japanese term "karoshi," which means "death by overwork," gained international attention when multiple cases emerged of workers suffering fatal heart attacks or strokes after consistently working more than 100 hours of overtime per month.[12] This tragic reality illustrates the extreme consequences that high-achieving cultures can have on individuals when burnout is left unchecked.

The rise of burnout in high-achieving cultures serves as a wake-up call, urging us to reconsider our relationship with work, productivity, and success. As we push ourselves to achieve more, the cost is increasingly being paid with our health, happiness, and overall sense of fulfillment. Recognizing and addressing burnout is crucial for individual well-being and building sustainable and thriving organizations.

While burnout manifests in physical exhaustion, the deeper cost is often emotional. After achieving the long-sought success, many are left with a sense of emptiness—the feeling that even with all the accolades, something vital is still missing. This is because, in the pursuit of success, many sacrifice their internal peace. The pursuit becomes about checking off milestones, and when those are achieved, there is little time spent savoring the present moment or enjoying personal fulfillment.

The Imbalance Between Success and Peace

This imbalance between success and inner peace is at the heart of the problem. Too often, we chase the next goal, believing it will bring us happiness, only to find that peace remains elusive. Like runners on a 'hedonic treadmill,' we chase achievements in the belief they'll bring lasting happiness, only to find ourselves stuck in an endless loop of fleeting satisfaction. It creates a cycle of striving that leaves us perpetually unfulfilled, as each new success only raises the bar, pushing true happiness further out of reach.

Success, as society defines it, asks us to constantly look forward—to the next promotion, the next project, the next achievement—while peace asks us to look inward, to cultivate a sense of fulfillment that is not dependent on external outcomes. From a young age, we are conditioned to equate success with external achievements—high grades, prestigious job titles, or material possessions. Social media amplifies this pressure by showcasing curated highlights of others' accomplishments, making us believe that we can only find happiness through constant achievement. As a result, we seldom question whether these external markers truly reflect our personal values or bring us genuine joy.

When these two forces are not in harmony, we find ourselves burned out, stressed, and questioning the actual value of our accomplishments. However, when we learn to harmonize success with inner peace, we discover a more sustainable path to fulfillment. By practicing mindfulness and gratitude, we shift our focus from what's next to appreciating what we have now. This shift allows us to pursue our ambitions from a place of wholeness, where each achievement feels like an authentic expression of our values rather than an endless pursuit of validation.

By embracing this approach, we open the door to a new way of living—one where ambition and inner peace not only coexist but also complement and strengthen each other. This journey is at the heart of what this book seeks to explore.

A New Approach: Balance Between Success and Peace

This book offers a new perspective: what if true success isn't just about reaching external milestones, but finding balance—where ambition and inner peace coexist? Instead of pushing yourself to exhaustion, you can redefine success to include your emotional well-being, allowing peace to guide your actions as you pursue your goals.

The core idea of this book is simple but powerful: success and peace are not mutually exclusive. When we stop seeing them as separate or opposing forces and instead work toward harmonizing them, we achieve more sustainably and live more fulfilling lives. Through mindfulness, intentional goal setting, and a shift in perspective, you can experience a kind of success that doesn't come at the cost of your inner peace but is enhanced by it.

By integrating practices that promote calm, self-awareness, and balance, you can approach your ambitions from a place of wholeness rather than stress. This book will guide you on reframing your goals, building resilience, and most importantly, maintaining a sense of peace throughout your journey. Whether you're striving for career growth, financial security, or personal development, the path forward doesn't have to involve burnout. Instead, it can be one where peace fuels your success, allowing both to thrive.

The Power of Inner Peace in the Pursuit of Success

Success is often defined by external achievements—wealth, status, and accomplishments. However, many successful individuals have discovered that true fulfillment requires inner peace and mindfulness. For example, Arianna Huffington, founder of HuffPost, realized the importance of well-being after collapsing from exhaustion in 2007. She redefined success by incorporating rest, mindfulness, and self-care into her life and business, ultimately launching Thrive Global, a platform focused on wellness.

Similarly, Ray Dalio, founder of Bridgewater Associates, credits his daily meditation practice with helping him manage the pressures of running a hedge fund. Through meditation, Dalio found clarity and emotional balance, which became key to his success.

Media mogul Oprah Winfrey has consistently advocated for the importance of inner peace and mindfulness. Growing up with hardships, she eventually found balance and purpose through meditation and gratitude practices, which she has openly shared through her platform *Super Soul Sunday*.

Even Steve Jobs, the visionary behind Apple, sought spiritual enlightenment through Zen Buddhism. His meditation practice helped him remain centered and calm, allowing him to push creative boundaries in the tech world.

These stories illustrate that success without inner peace can be unsustainable. Incorporating mindfulness and self-care not only enhances personal well-being but also leads to more balanced, long-lasting success.

A Roadmap for Balance: The Flow of This Book

Welcome to a journey where success no longer requires sacrificing your well-being. In The Quiet Hustle, we'll challenge the myth that endless striving and hustle are the only ways to achieve meaningful success. Instead, this book will guide you toward a life where ambition and peace work hand in hand.

We begin by debunking the myth of hustle culture—the belief that working harder, faster, and longer is the ultimate path to success. This mentality is often praised in society, but it leads to burnout, stress, and a sense of dissatisfaction. You'll learn why this approach is unsustainable and how redefining success can create room for fulfillment and balance.

Next, we delve into the concept of inner peace—why it's essential, and how to cultivate it in your daily life. Through mindfulness and intentional living, you'll discover how to maintain a sense of calm even while pursuing your goals. The key is not to give up your ambitions but to approach them from a place of grounded peace.

We'll then move into the practical steps for aligning your ambition with well-being. You'll explore strategies for setting goals that resonate with your core values, managing time and energy without losing yourself, and keeping your peace intact as you work toward your aspirations.

However, with ambition often comes self-doubt. That's why we confront impostor syndrome, that persistent voice inside that questions your worth and makes you feel like a fraud, no matter how much you achieve. This section will teach you how to overcome impostor syndrome, freeing yourself from the fear that you don't deserve your success and empowering you to move forward with confidence.

Once we address those internal barriers, we'll focus on the interplay between success and peace. We'll explore how these two forces can coexist harmoniously, challenging the idea that success must come at the expense of your peace of mind. You'll see how balancing ambition with inner calm creates a more sustainable, fulfilling path forward.

Next, we dive into resilience—your ability to navigate setbacks and grow from adversity. Life will throw challenges your way, but you'll learn how to rise, adapt, and continue your journey without losing your sense of calm or direction. Resilience is the bedrock of success and peace, helping you move forward even in the face of hardship.

Once you've built resilience, we'll turn to the quiet power of patience. In a world that prizes speed and instant results, patience can feel counterintuitive, but it is one of the most crucial traits for long-term success. You'll discover how to develop patience with yourself, your goals, and life's timing—understanding that true growth and success take time to cultivate.

As the journey progresses, we'll explore the importance of embracing imperfection. Real success isn't about being flawless; it's about embracing your humanity and continuing to move forward despite setbacks. You'll learn how to practice self-compassion, letting go of the unrealistic need to be perfect, and instead, focus on growth and progress.

Finally, we'll conclude with the practices of gratitude and letting go. Gratitude allows you to shift your focus from scarcity to abundance, and learning to let go of control over outcomes frees you from unnecessary stress. Together, these practices enhance both your peace and your success, helping you approach life with greater freedom and joy.

This book is not just about achieving more—it's about achieving a life that nourishes both your external success and your inner well-being.

Through these principles, you'll learn to redefine success, find balance, and thrive without losing yourself in the process.

A Journey Worth Taking

The path to success doesn't have to be one of stress, burnout, and sacrifice. You can have both—a fulfilling life marked by peace, and the achievements you've always dreamed of. But it requires a shift in how you define success and how you approach the journey. As you turn the page, ask yourself: What would your life look like if, instead of chasing success, you allowed success to come from a place of calm, clarity, and balance? Imagine a version of yourself that no longer must choose between ambition and peace—where both thrive together.

Are you ready to embark on a journey where your ambition and inner peace don't have to be at odds? The path awaits, and this book is your guide.

Ethan's Journey Begins

Ethan, a successful marketing executive, found himself overwhelmed by the relentless demands of hustle culture. *As he raced through his days, achieving one milestone after another, a sense of discontent lingered beneath the surface. In search of a deeper fulfillment, he began to question the true meaning of success.*

This book invites you to join Ethan on his transformative journey—a quest for balance between ambition and inner peace. Through his experiences, we will explore themes of resilience, gratitude, and the importance of embracing imperfections, uncovering practical strategies for cultivating a fulfilling life.

One

$\text{\textsection}$

The Myth of the "Hustle Culture"

It was 6 a.m. when Ethan's alarm blared, pulling him from a restless sleep. As he fumbled to silence it, a wave of anxiety washed over him at the sight of countless notifications on his phone. Emails from clients, reminders about meetings, and messages from his team filled the screen. The demands of his job as a marketing executive felt overwhelming, and the pressure to succeed loomed larger with each passing day.

As he poured himself a cup of coffee, Ethan gazed out the window, watching the world awaken. He had always believed that success was defined by ambition and relentless effort, a mindset ingrained in him since childhood. Yet, lately, he felt a growing sense of unease. Was this endless hustle truly fulfilling? Despite his achievements—promotions, accolades, and a busy social life—Ethan often found himself questioning whether he was genuinely happy.

The more he pushed himself, the more he felt the weight of exhaustion. His friends praised his work ethic, often calling him a "go-getter," but beneath that label lay a deep-seated fatigue. He found himself racing through life, constantly striving for the next milestone, only to discover that the finish line kept shifting. Each success felt fleeting, leaving him feeling empty and burned out.

Today, as he prepared for yet another demanding day, Ethan made a decision: it was time to reassess his relationship with hustle culture. He wanted to challenge the notion that constant striving equated to success. Could there be another way? Was it possible to redefine his understanding of achievement to include his mental and emotional well-being?

With a flicker of determination, Ethan resolved to embark on a journey of self-discovery—a quest for balance between his ambitions and the inner peace he had long neglected. Little did he know, this journey would not only transform his perspective but also reshape his entire approach to life and success.

Introduction: The Perpetual Grind

It's 6 a.m., and your alarm jolts you awake. You check your phone—emails, missed calls, messages—all demanding your attention before you've even gotten out of bed. By the time you've had your first sip of coffee, you're already racing through the day, planning, strategizing, checking off to-do lists. In our fast-paced, hyper-connected world, this scene has become the norm for millions of people striving to "make it." We wear exhaustion like a badge of honor, equating busy schedules and constant striving with success.

But is this relentless hustle actually bringing us closer to fulfillment? Or are we simply running on a treadmill, mistaking constant motion for meaningful progress?

For years, society has glorified the hustle—endless productivity, sleepless nights, and a laser focus on climbing the ladder. We're told to keep pushing, keep grinding, and never stop, no matter the cost. Yet, amid the race to achieve more, many are left feeling burnt out, disconnected, and unfulfilled.

This chapter will challenge the myth that constant hustle is the key to success and explore the idea that mindful work and intentional living offer a more sustainable path toward true achievement.

The Rise of Hustle Culture

Over the past decade, hustle culture has seeped into nearly every facet of our lives. From social media influencers posting their #RiseAndGrind routines to entrepreneurial icons urging us to "outwork everyone," the message is clear: if you aren't hustling 24/7, you're falling behind. This constant push to be productive has become so ingrained in our daily lives that it's no longer just a mindset—it's a societal expectation.

Social media has played a significant role in amplifying this phenomenon. Platforms like Instagram, Twitter, and LinkedIn have become showcases for relentless ambition, with individuals sharing their achievements, side hustles, and "no days off" attitudes. We're constantly bombarded with images of people working late into the night, celebrating promotions, or launching new projects, often accompanied by undertones implying success requires never-ending effort. This constant exposure creates an illusion that everyone is always on the grind, making us feel as though we must keep up or risk being left behind.

The rise of technology and the always-on culture have blurred the lines between work and rest. Smartphones and laptops have made it possible to work from anywhere, at any time. What used to be confined to the office now follows us home, to the gym, and even on vacation. As a result, the pressure to be productive extends beyond traditional work hours, leaving little room for relaxation or self-care. We find ourselves checking emails during dinner, answering work calls on weekends, or feeling guilty if we're not actively pursuing our goals.

Entrepreneurial leaders and motivational speakers have also contributed to the glorification of hustle culture. We idolize figures like Elon Musk, who famously advocates for 80-hour workweeks,[13] or Gary Vaynerchuk, who champions the idea that every spare minute should be used to pursue success.[14] While their messages are intended to inspire, they often create unrealistic expectations, leading us to believe that unless we're sacrificing sleep, leisure, and personal time, we're not doing enough. This mindset can be especially harmful, as it disregards the need for balance and self-care, promoting burnout as a necessary step toward success.

Even the concept of self-worth has become entangled with productivity, with phrases like "I'll sleep when I'm dead" or "grind now, shine later" reinforcing the idea that our value is tied to how much we can achieve. This glorification of busyness has made it socially acceptable—even admirable—to neglect our health, relationships, and well-being in the name of progress. It's no longer enough to be good at what we do; we must be exceptional, tireless, and perpetually striving for more.

However, this relentless pursuit of success often comes at a cost. As we chase after the ideals presented by hustle culture, we risk losing touch with what truly matters—our mental health, our connections with others, and our sense of inner peace. Studies have shown that chronic exposure to this mindset can lead to increased levels of stress, anxiety, and even depression, as we continuously compare ourselves to others and feel pressure to achieve more.[15]

Ultimately, the danger of hustle culture lies in its unspoken assumption that rest is a sign of weakness, and that self-worth is measured by productivity alone. But if we step back, we can begin to challenge this narrative and redefine what success means on our terms—where ambition and well-being can coexist, and where taking time to rest, reflect, and recharge is seen as a strength, not a setback.

The Invisible Cost of Always Hustling

The relentless pressure to hustle comes with a steep price: our well-being. In our quest for success, the idea that we must always be "on" has become ingrained in our culture, but this mindset is unsustainable and often leads to severe consequences. Research shows that chronic stress and overwork lead to burnout, affecting our mental, emotional, and even physical health.[16] The emotional exhaustion, cynicism, and decreased sense of accomplishment are all symptoms of a deeper issue—one that hustle culture conveniently overlooks.

The Physical Toll

One study conducted by the World Health Organization found that overworking is linked to a significant increase in the risk of heart disease and stroke.[17] The constant pressure to perform, meet deadlines, and exceed expectations triggers the body's stress response, flooding the system with hormones like cortisol and adrenaline. While these hormones can be helpful in short bursts, prolonged exposure can lead to serious health problems such as high blood pressure, weakened immune function, and even digestive issues.[18] In extreme cases, this can result in what the Japanese call "karoshi," or death from overwork, highlighting that the physical risks of hustle culture are not only real but potentially life-threatening.

The Mental and Emotional Impact

But the risks aren't only physical. Overworking often causes individuals to become disconnected from their personal lives, passions, and, ultimately, themselves. This disconnection can lead to feelings of isolation, anxiety, and depression. According to a study published in the *Journal of Occupational Health Psychology*, individuals who frequently engage in overwork are more likely to experience symptoms of anxiety and depression, largely due to the lack of downtime needed to process emotions and recharge. [19] The constant hustle leaves little room for reflection, self-care, or the pursuit of activities that bring genuine joy, creating a vicious cycle where people feel trapped in their work without any sense of purpose or fulfillment.

Relationships and Social Life Suffer

Hustle culture doesn't just affect our internal world—it also impacts the people around us. When we're consumed by work, we have less time and energy to invest in our relationships. Friendships become neglected, family time is sacrificed, and meaningful connections are replaced by endless meetings, emails, and tasks. A study from the *Harvard Business Review* revealed that individuals who work excessive hours are more likely to experience strained relationships and higher rates of loneliness.[20] This social isolation further exacerbates the negative effects of burnout, as humans are inherently social beings who thrive on connection and support.[21]

The Myth of Productivity

Ironically, the pursuit of constant productivity often results in diminished efficiency over time. As we push ourselves to work longer hours, the quality of our work declines, creativity wanes, and problem-solving abilities diminish. A Stanford University study found that productivity per hour declines sharply after a 50-hour workweek, and those who work up to 70 hours accomplish little more than their 50-hour counterparts.[22] This means that the extra hours spent hustling don't translate into meaningful gains—they simply lead to exhaustion, mistakes, and a growing sense of frustration.

The Erosion of Identity and Passion

Perhaps the most insidious cost of hustle culture is how it erodes our sense of identity. When we define ourselves solely by our achievements and productivity, we lose sight of who we are beyond our work. Passions, hobbies, and personal growth take a back seat to professional ambitions, leaving us feeling empty and unfulfilled once the temporary high of success fades. Over time, this can lead to a profound sense of disillusionment, as we realize that the things we've sacrificed—our health, relationships, and personal growth—are the very things that bring meaning and joy to our lives.

Finding Balance

While ambition and hard work have their place, the invisible costs of always hustling remind us that a more balanced approach to success is not only healthier but also more sustainable. True fulfillment comes from finding harmony between work and life, allowing us to pursue our goals without sacrificing our well-being in the process. By redefining success to include time for rest, reflection, and connection, we can begin to dismantle the damaging effects of hustle culture and create a more fulfilling path forward.

What Are We Really Chasing?

Perhaps the most deceptive aspect of hustle culture is the illusion of what's waiting at the finish line. We're often promised that once we "make it"—whether that means hitting a six-figure salary, earning a prestigious title, or becoming widely recognized—our sense of worth and happiness will fall neatly into place. But this belief is a carefully constructed mirage, and too often, when we reach these milestones, we find ourselves feeling emptier than before, left with the unsettling question: *"Is this really all there is?"*

The problem lies in the story we've been sold. Hustle culture has convinced us that our value is intrinsically tied to our productivity, that we are only as worthy as our last achievement or our latest success. It reduces our identities to what we can prove, what we can accumulate, and how tirelessly we can work, until there's no distinction between who we are and what we do. In this relentless pursuit, we become strangers to ourselves, forever chasing an ever-elusive sense of validation.

This mindset leaves little room for internal growth, self-reflection, or genuine contentment. By focusing solely on external markers of success, we neglect the quieter, more meaningful aspects of life—the connections we build, the passions we nurture, and the inner peace we cultivate when we're not racing against the clock. In the end, the finish line is a mirage, constantly shifting, always demanding more, and never offering the fulfillment it promised. It's only when we step off the treadmill that we begin to realize that true success isn't about what we achieve but about the person we become along the way.

Mindful Work vs. Mindless Hustle

The good news is there's an alternative: mindful work. Mindfulness doesn't mean giving up on your ambitions or working less; it means working with intention and awareness. It's about creating a life where success is defined by more than just output and external validation. When we approach our work mindfully, we become more attuned to why we're doing what we're doing. We begin to align our daily actions with our values, allowing our work to become a source of fulfillment rather than a source of stress.

Mindful work is also about recognizing when to pause, when to reflect, and when to prioritize self-care. It teaches us that sometimes, stepping back is the most productive thing we can do. As the saying goes, "You can't pour from an empty cup." Learning to protect your peace and well-being is not a weakness—it's a strength that will sustain you for the long haul.

Action Step: Assessing Your Current Pace

Before we continue, take a moment to reflect on your own relationship with hustle culture. Are you constantly in a state of striving, rarely pausing to enjoy the present? Or have you found ways to balance your drive with moments of peace and reflection?

Here's an exercise to help you assess your current pace:

1. **Time Audit**: Over the next week, track how you spend your time, both at work and in your personal life. Are you filling every moment with tasks? Do you feel guilty when you're not working? How often do you pause to rest, reflect, or recharge?

2. **Work-Life Satisfaction Scale**: Rate your current work-life balance on a scale from 1 to 10 (1 being completely off-balance and 10 being perfectly balanced). What would it take to move your rating up one point?

3. **Pause for Reflection**: Take 10 minutes today to sit quietly, free of distractions. Consider how you want to feel about your work and life a year from now. What small shifts can you make today to move closer to that vision?

Summary: The Myth of the "Hustle Culture"

In this chapter, we examined the rise of hustle culture and the societal pressures that glorify constant productivity, relentless striving, and the pursuit of success at any cost. While hustle culture promises achievement and fulfillment, it often results in burnout, exhaustion, and a deep sense of emptiness. The chapter reveals the invisible costs of always hustling, such as the impact on mental, emotional, and physical health, and how it disconnects us from genuine happiness, purpose, and the people who matter most.

The chapter challenges readers to question the traditional notion of success and encourages them to redefine it in a way that includes both achievement and inner peace. Introducing mindful work as an alternative to mindless hustle emphasizes that sustainable success is about aligning your efforts with your true values and finding joy in the process, rather than constantly chasing external validation.

Key Takeaways

- Hustle culture often leads to burnout, stress, and a never-ending cycle of striving, ultimately preventing us from experiencing true fulfillment.

- True success isn't about constant productivity but about balancing ambition with inner peace, enabling a more intentional, purposeful journey.

- Mindful work allows you to reconnect with what matters most, helping you pursue your goals with clarity, authenticity, and a sense of meaning.

Conclusion: Choosing a Different Path

The hustle will always be tempting. It's loud, it's flashy, and it promises quick results. But there's another way forward—one that's quieter, slower, and more intentional. It's a path that values presence over productivity, meaning over metrics.

As we continue this journey, we'll explore how you can redefine success on your own terms, integrating ambition with peace to create a life that feels fulfilling, not just busy. It starts with the courage to step away from the grind and embrace a new way of working—a way that honors both your goals and your well-being.

Two

꧁

Defining Inner Peace

Ethan sat at his kitchen table, the weight of his daily responsibilities pressing down on him. *The to-do lists, reports, and meetings had been constants in his life for years, symbols of his relentless pursuit of success. Yet something had shifted since the moment he made a commitment to change—a commitment to discover a deeper sense of fulfillment and balance.*

It wasn't long ago that Ethan decided to take a step back from the hustle that had defined his life. He had been driven by the belief that constant effort and achievement were the only paths to success, but that mindset had left him burned out, detached, and unsatisfied. Now, on this new journey of self-discovery, Ethan knew there had to be a better way. But how?

One concept that kept appearing in his research and conversations was "inner peace." At first, the idea seemed foreign, even contradictory, to the world he had known. He was accustomed to pushing through challenges, not slowing down to find calm in the middle of them. But as he dug deeper, Ethan began to wonder if inner peace might be the missing part in his pursuit—not as a retreat from ambition, but as a way to align it with well-being.

He decided to take the first steps. Tentatively, Ethan downloaded a meditation app, though the idea of sitting still felt almost like a guilty pleasure. But after years of running at full speed, even just a few minutes of mindfulness each morning started to change something within him. The moments of stillness felt awkward at first, yet strangely necessary— like giving his mind a chance to catch up with his life.

As days passed, Ethan noticed subtle shifts. His reaction to stress softened; he was more thoughtful in his responses to challenges. The constant pressure that once dominated his thoughts began to ease, replaced by a growing curiosity about this new way of being. He realized that inner peace wasn't about escaping or avoiding the demands of life but learning to carry a sense of calm within him as he faced them.

It became clear to him that inner peace could coexist with his ambition. It wasn't about abandoning his goals or giving up on success. Instead, it was about approaching his aspirations with a balanced mindset—one that allowed room for both drive and tranquility. Slowly, Ethan began to understand that real success wasn't just measured by external achievements, but by how centered he felt within himself.

The journey wasn't easy, and old habits continued to linger. But with each step, Ethan grew more confident that inner peace was something he could nurture, even in the most hectic moments. It was no longer a distant, abstract idea—it was becoming a part of him.

Introduction: What Is Inner Peace, Really?

When we hear the term "inner peace," it often conjures images of monks meditating on mountaintops or people finding brief moments of calm in a chaotic world. But inner peace is more than just a fleeting moment of tranquility—it's a state of being. It's an ongoing process of maintaining balance, resilience, and clarity, even in the face of challenges.

In this chapter, we'll explore what inner peace really means, why it's essential for long-term fulfillment, and how cultivating it can enhance not only your well-being but also your ability to achieve your goals.

The Misconceptions About Inner Peace

Many people mistakenly believe that inner peace equates to a state of perpetual calmness or a life devoid of challenges. This perception can be misleading and even discouraging, as it sets an unrealistic expectation that life should be entirely smooth, and that any turbulence signifies a failure to maintain peace. In reality, inner peace isn't about eliminating stress or discomfort—it's about navigating through them with grace and resilience. It's not about shutting the world out but engaging with it from a place of grounded strength.

One of the most common misconceptions is that inner peace is synonymous with passivity, as if achieving it means retreating from ambition or surrendering your goals. However, inner peace is not about avoiding life's demands or shrinking from your aspirations; it's about cultivating a state of mind that allows you to face life's challenges with clarity and purpose. Rather than being a state of inaction, inner peace empowers you to act with greater intention and presence. It's the calm center from which you can make decisions, take risks, and pursue your ambitions without being overwhelmed by external pressures.

Another misconception is that inner peace is a final destination, something you either have or don't have. In truth, inner peace is an ongoing practice—a dynamic journey rather than a fixed state. It ebbs and flows, influenced by the ups and downs of daily life. Some days, you may feel deeply connected to that sense of calm, while on others, it may seem elusive. This variability is natural and does not mean you've lost your sense of peace; rather, it's an invitation to continually return to practices that ground and center you.

Inner peace is also often misunderstood as a solitary pursuit, as if it requires withdrawing from others to maintain. While moments of solitude can be valuable, true inner peace enables you to be fully present in your relationships, work, and community. It allows you to engage with the world from a place of authenticity and compassion, fostering deeper connections with others because the need for external validation or approval no longer drives you.

In essence, inner peace is not about escaping the world but about meeting it with a sense of balance and equanimity. It's about developing the inner strength to remain steady amidst life's storms rather than being swept away by them. By cultivating this mindset, you're better equipped to face obstacles, adapt to change, and pursue your goals with passion and patience. When you understand that inner peace is an active, evolving process, it becomes the foundation upon which sustainable success is built.

What Inner Peace Really Is: The Three Pillars

To truly understand inner peace, it's helpful to break it down into three interconnected pillars that form its foundation. Each of these elements contributes to cultivating a state of calm, clarity, and resilience, allowing you to navigate life's challenges with greater ease.

Emotional Regulation

Emotional regulation is the ability to manage your emotions in a way that keeps you grounded, especially during stressful or challenging situations. Inner peace doesn't mean you won't feel negative emotions—such as anger, sadness, or frustration—but rather that you can acknowledge these emotions without letting them dictate your actions. It's about creating space between stimulus and response, giving yourself the chance to choose a more thoughtful and constructive reaction.

Imagine a situation where you receive criticism at work. Instead of reacting defensively or allowing your self-esteem to plummet, emotional regulation enables you to pause, process the feedback, and respond with curiosity rather than defensiveness. This practice requires self-awareness and the willingness to confront uncomfortable feelings, but over time, it becomes easier to manage emotions without being controlled by them.

Practical Insight: When you feel overwhelmed, take a moment to label your emotions. Are you feeling anxious, frustrated, or disappointed? By simply naming your feelings, you gain a sense of control over them, making it easier to choose how you respond. This small act of acknowledgment can prevent your emotions from snowballing and help you maintain inner peace.

Mindfulness

Mindfulness is the practice of being fully present in each moment, without judgment or distraction. It goes beyond just meditation—it's about cultivating an awareness of your thoughts, feelings, and surroundings in everyday life. When you practice mindfulness, you create a sense of inner calm that enables you to navigate life's complexities with greater intention and clarity.

For example, think about how often you go through your day on autopilot—rushing through tasks, conversations, or even meals without truly being present. Mindfulness invites you to slow down and engage fully with whatever you're doing, whether it's a work project, a conversation, or a quiet moment alone. This heightened awareness helps you make choices that align with your values, rather than being swept away by distractions or impulses.

Practical Insight: Incorporate mindfulness into your daily routine by choosing one activity to do mindfully each day. It could be as simple as savoring your morning coffee, paying attention to the flavors, aroma, and warmth, or fully listening to a colleague during a conversation without thinking about your to-do list. These moments of presence add up, gradually training your mind to find peace amidst the chaos.

Resilience

Resilience is the capacity to bounce back from adversity, setbacks, or unexpected challenges without losing your sense of inner peace. It's not about avoiding difficulties but rather about facing them with a mindset that turns obstacles into opportunities for growth. Resilience helps you maintain your equilibrium even when life throws you off course, allowing you to adapt and persevere.

Consider a time when you faced a major setback, such as a career disappointment, a failed relationship, or a personal loss. In these moments, resilience isn't about pretending everything is fine; it's about acknowledging the pain and choosing to keep moving forward despite it. This pillar of inner peace encourages you to see challenges as temporary and surmountable, giving you the strength to continue your journey with courage and optimism.

Practical Insight: When you encounter setbacks, practice asking yourself, *"What can I learn from this?"* By shifting your focus from what went wrong to what you can gain from the experience, you train your mind to see challenges as growth opportunities rather than threats. This mindset shift builds your resilience and strengthens your inner peace.

The Harmony of the Three Pillars

The true power of inner peace lies not in any single pillar but in the dynamic interplay between emotional regulation, mindfulness, and resilience. These three components are deeply interconnected, each one reinforcing and amplifying the others to create a balanced, harmonious state of being.

When you become skilled at regulating your emotions, you create a calmer internal environment that makes it easier to practice mindfulness. You're less likely to be swept away by a flood of emotions, allowing you to stay present in the moment. For example, if you receive difficult feedback at work, emotional regulation helps you acknowledge your initial feelings without being overwhelmed. This emotional steadiness allows you to remain mindful of your thoughts and responses rather than reacting impulsively.

As mindfulness becomes a regular part of your life, it enhances your resilience by allowing you to observe challenges with greater clarity and perspective. When you're fully present, you can face setbacks without being consumed by them. You begin to see obstacles not as insurmountable walls but as opportunities for growth and learning. This awareness enables you to bounce back more quickly, as you're less likely to take setbacks personally or view them as reflections of your worth.

Resilience, in turn, strengthens both emotional regulation and mindfulness. Each time you navigate a challenge, you build confidence in your ability to handle whatever life throws your way. This resilience creates a sense of inner stability, making it easier to regulate your emotions the next time you encounter stress. It also fosters a deeper mindfulness practice, as you learn to stay present even in difficult circumstances, trusting that you have the strength to persevere.

Consider a moment when life feels overwhelming—perhaps a sudden change disrupts your plans, or you face an unexpected challenge that shakes your confidence. In such moments, these three pillars work together seamlessly. Your emotional regulation allows you to acknowledge and process your feelings without being consumed by them. Mindfulness keeps you grounded, enabling you to focus on what you can control in the present moment. Resilience helps you adapt, finding ways to move forward despite the uncertainty. It's this harmony that transforms inner peace from a concept into a lived experience.

By embracing all three pillars, you develop the ability to respond to life's circumstances with purpose, clarity, and grace. Instead of being reactive or caught up in cycles of stress and frustration, you approach challenges with a calm, centered mindset. This doesn't mean you won't encounter difficulties—life will always present obstacles—but it does mean you'll face them from a place of inner strength and confidence.

The Ripple Effect on Ambition and Success

When emotional regulation, mindfulness, and resilience work together, they do more than create a sense of inner calm; they become catalysts for personal growth and success. As you cultivate these qualities, you'll notice profound changes in how you approach your goals and ambitions. Decisions become more intentional, relationships more authentic, and setbacks less daunting.

For instance, instead of allowing a project's setbacks to derail your motivation, you might use mindfulness to stay present, focusing on what can be learned or adjusted. Emotional regulation keeps you from spiraling into self-doubt, while resilience helps you adapt your strategies and keep moving forward. This ability to navigate challenges gracefully is often the difference between those who give up when faced with obstacles and those who continue to grow and succeed.

Practical Ways to Strengthen the Harmony

Achieving balance between ambition and inner peace requires more than just understanding the concepts of emotional regulation, mindfulness, and resilience—it involves actively practicing them in daily life. The following strategies are simple yet effective ways to strengthen this harmony. By integrating these practices, you can enhance self-awareness, reframe challenges, and cultivate mindfulness, allowing you to approach life's demands with clarity, calm, and strength. Let these tools support your journey toward a more peaceful and fulfilling life.

1. **Practice Mindful Emotional Check-ins:** Set aside a few moments each day to check in with your emotions. Ask yourself: *"What am I feeling right now?"* and *"How are these feelings affecting my thoughts and actions?"* This simple exercise helps you regulate your

emotions and strengthens your mindfulness by bringing you into the present moment.

2. **Embrace Challenges as Opportunities for Growth:** When faced with a difficult situation, take a step back and view it through the lens of resilience. Ask yourself, *"What can I learn from this?"* or *"How can this experience make me stronger?"* By framing challenges as opportunities, you reinforce the idea that setbacks are not roadblocks but stepping stones to personal growth.

3. **Cultivate Daily Mindfulness Habits:** Whether it's through meditation, mindful breathing, or simply being present during everyday activities, integrating mindfulness into your routine creates a solid foundation for emotional regulation and resilience. The more you practice, the easier it becomes to maintain inner peace, even in the face of stress.

4. **Reflect on Past Experiences:** Take time to reflect on past challenges and how you've grown from them. Notice how you regulated your emotions, practiced mindfulness, or demonstrated resilience. This reflection reinforces the interconnectedness of the three pillars and builds your confidence in applying them to future situations.

A Lifelong Journey Toward Inner Peace

The journey to inner peace is not a destination but a continuous process of integrating these three pillars into your life. As you develop emotional regulation, mindfulness, and resilience, they become second nature—tools you can draw upon instinctively in any situation. Over time, you'll find that life's inevitable ups and downs no longer disrupt your sense of inner calm but instead become opportunities to deepen your practice and strengthen your inner peace.

By harnessing the harmony of these pillars, you're not just cultivating a state of inner peace; you're building a foundation for a life that aligns with your values, aspirations, and true self. This harmony between your internal world and external ambitions creates a powerful sense of fulfillment and allows you to pursue success without sacrificing your well-being.

Why Inner Peace Is Essential for Success

Success without inner peace is often hollow. While you might achieve impressive goals and accumulate accolades, the sense of satisfaction can be fleeting if it's not grounded in a deeper sense of fulfillment. This is why so many high achievers, despite reaching the pinnacles of their careers, still find themselves yearning for something more—an unshakable feeling that something is missing. Inner peace fills that gap, offering a path to a more profound and sustainable form of success.

When you cultivate inner peace, you're no longer solely driven by external validation or the constant chase for more. Instead, you create space for reflection, creativity, and authentic growth. This shift allows you to pursue your ambitions from a place of abundance rather than scarcity, enabling you to make decisions that align with your true values and goals.

Inner Peace Creates Clarity and Better Decision-Making

One of the most significant ways inner peace contributes to success is by providing mental clarity. When you're at peace with yourself, you're less likely to be swayed by fear, anxiety, or the pressure to conform to others' expectations. Instead of making impulsive decisions based on stress or external demands, you respond thoughtfully, guided by your core values and long-term vision.

For example, imagine someone facing a career crossroads. Without inner peace, they might feel pressured to choose the most prestigious or lucrative option, even if it doesn't align with their passions or values. However, when grounded in inner peace, they can make a more authentic decision, one that honors their true aspirations and leads to a more fulfilling path.

Practical Insight: When faced with a tough decision, take a few moments to breathe deeply and center yourself. Ask, "Is this choice aligned with my values and vision?" This simple practice helps you tap into your inner peace and make decisions that are more likely to lead to lasting success.

Inner Peace Enhances Relationships and Leadership

Success is rarely achieved in isolation; it often requires collaboration, communication, and the ability to inspire others. Inner peace equips you with the emotional intelligence needed to connect with others on a deeper level, making you a more effective leader, colleague, or partner. When you're at peace with yourself, you're less likely to react defensively or be triggered by others' opinions or actions. Instead, you respond with empathy, understanding, and authenticity.

For instance, consider a team leader who encounters conflict within their team. A leader lacking inner peace might respond with frustration or take sides, escalating tensions. However, a leader grounded in inner peace can approach the situation calmly, listen to each perspective, and facilitate a resolution that fosters trust and collaboration. This ability to navigate interpersonal challenges with grace is a hallmark of effective and impactful leadership.

Practical Insight: Next time you face a challenging interaction, practice pausing before you respond. Take a breath and approach the situation with curiosity rather than judgment. This simple act can transform your relationships and strengthen your leadership presence.

Inner Peace Fuels Creativity and Innovation

When your mind is cluttered with stress and anxiety, creativity often takes a backseat. Inner peace, however, allows you to tap into a state of flow where ideas emerge more freely and intuitively. In this state, your mind is open to new possibilities, connections, and insights that might otherwise be overlooked.

For example, many professionals experience creative breakthroughs when they step away from their desks—during a walk, a shower, or even while cooking a meal. These moments of relaxation

43

allow the mind to wander, making space for creative insights to surface. This demonstrates that when you cultivate inner peace, you're more likely to access the creative potential needed for innovation and problem-solving.

Scientific Insight: A study published in the journal Psychological Science found that mindfulness meditation improves divergent thinking, a key component of creativity. [23] When you're at peace with your thoughts, your brain is more capable of generating original ideas, making connections between seemingly unrelated concepts, and approaching problems from fresh perspectives. This ability to innovate is often what sets truly successful individuals apart in their fields.

Inner Peace Builds Resilience and Sustains Long-Term Success

The path to success is rarely linear. It's filled with setbacks, obstacles, and unexpected challenges. Inner peace equips you with the resilience needed to navigate these difficulties without losing your sense of purpose or direction. When you're grounded in inner peace, you're more likely to view setbacks as temporary and manageable, rather than as insurmountable roadblocks.

Consider a professional who loses a major client or misses out on a promotion. Without inner peace, they might spiral into self-doubt or question their abilities. However, with inner peace, they're able to accept the setback, reflect on what they can learn from the experience, and approach future opportunities with renewed confidence and determination. This resilience not only helps them bounce back but also positions them for greater success in the long run.

Practical Insight: When you encounter setbacks, take time to reflect on what you've learned rather than dwelling on the disappointment. This shift in perspective helps build resilience and keeps you moving forward on your path to success.

Inner Peace Redefines Success on Your Own Terms

Perhaps most importantly, inner peace allows you to define success on your own terms. Instead of chasing societal definitions of achievement—such as status, wealth, or fame—you focus on what genuinely matters to you. This shift from external validation to internal fulfillment transforms the way you approach your goals, ensuring that the success you pursue is deeply aligned with your values and aspirations.

When you find inner peace, you measure your achievements not by how they compare to others but by how they resonate with your true self. This redefined sense of success brings a profound sense of contentment and satisfaction, allowing you to celebrate your journey rather than constantly striving for the next milestone.

Practical Insight: Regularly check in with yourself by asking, *"What does success look like for me right now?"* This question helps you stay connected to your inner peace and ensures that you're pursuing goals that genuinely align with your values.

The Profound Impact of Inner Peace on Success

Inner peace is not just a "nice-to-have" quality; it's foundational for achieving lasting and meaningful success. By nurturing clarity, enhancing relationships, fueling creativity, building resilience, and redefining success on your terms, inner peace becomes the guiding force that propels you forward. It shifts your mindset from one of striving and chasing to one of intentional, purpose-driven action.

As you continue your journey, remember that true success is not measured solely by the accolades you earn or the milestones you reach, but by the sense of fulfillment and peace you experience along the way. When inner peace is at the core of your pursuit, every step forward becomes an expression of who you truly are, making your achievements not only more impactful but also more deeply satisfying.

How to Cultivate Inner Peace

Cultivating inner peace is a lifelong journey, not a destination. It requires patience, intentionality, and a commitment to nurturing your mental, emotional, and spiritual well-being. While achieving inner peace doesn't happen overnight, there are simple yet powerful practices you can incorporate into your daily life that will help you take meaningful steps toward this state of balance and tranquility.

Daily Mindfulness Practice

Mindfulness is one of the most effective ways to cultivate inner peace, as it trains your mind to be present and aware of the moment without judgment. By dedicating just 5–10 minutes a day to mindfulness, you gradually develop the ability to observe your thoughts and emotions without being overwhelmed by them.

How to Practice: Find a quiet space where you won't be interrupted. Sit comfortably, close your eyes, and focus on your breath. As you breathe in and out, notice the sensations of the air entering and leaving your body. When your mind inevitably wanders—which it will—gently bring your focus back to your breath without frustration or judgment. This simple act of redirecting your attention helps train your mind to stay grounded in the present.

Practical Insight: If you find it difficult to sit in silence, consider using a guided meditation app or even engaging in a mindful activity such as walking, eating, or listening to music. The goal is not to empty your mind but to observe your thoughts without getting caught up in them.

Why It Works: Regular mindfulness practice strengthens your ability to respond to life's challenges with clarity and calm, rather than reacting impulsively or out of habit. Over time, it helps create a sense of inner peace that you can carry with you, even during stressful moments.

Emotional Check-Ins

One of the keys to inner peace is emotional regulation, and this starts with becoming more aware of how you're feeling throughout the day. By taking regular "emotional check-ins," you can identify when stress, frustration, or anxiety starts to build, giving you the opportunity to process these emotions before they escalate.

How to Practice: Set a reminder on your phone or place sticky notes in visible areas with the prompt: *"How am I feeling right now?"* When you notice the reminder, take a moment to pause, close your eyes, and tune into your body. Are you feeling tense? Anxious? Energized? Content? Simply acknowledging your emotions without judgment helps you gain control over them, rather than allowing them to control you.

Practical Insight: When you identify a negative emotion, take a few deep breaths and ask yourself, *"What do I need in this moment?"* This could be a quick walk, a chat with a friend, or even just a few moments of silence. By addressing your emotional needs, you create space for inner peace to grow.

Why It Works: Regular emotional check-ins help you develop self-awareness and emotional intelligence, which are essential for maintaining inner peace. Instead of suppressing or ignoring your feelings, you learn to process them in a healthy and constructive way.

Gratitude Practice

Gratitude is a powerful tool for cultivating inner peace because it shifts your focus from what you lack to what you already have. By regularly acknowledging the positive aspects of your life, you foster a mindset of abundance and contentment, which counteracts feelings of stress, anxiety, and dissatisfaction.

How to Practice: Each day, take a few minutes to write down three things you're grateful for. They can be as simple as a warm cup of coffee, a kind gesture from a colleague, or a moment of laughter with a friend. As you write, take a moment to fully feel the gratitude for each item.

Practical Insight: To deepen this practice, try focusing on a different theme each week—such as relationships, personal achievements, or the beauty of nature. This encourages you to expand your perspective and recognize sources of gratitude in all areas of your life.

Why It Works: Research has shown that regularly practicing gratitude can reduce stress, increase happiness, and improve overall well-being.[24] By fostering a grateful mindset, you create a more positive and peaceful inner world, regardless of external circumstances.

Set Boundaries

One of the greatest obstacles to inner peace is overcommitment. When you spread yourself too thin or allow others to dictate your time and energy, you become overwhelmed and stressed, making it difficult to maintain a sense of calm. Remembering to set healthy boundaries is crucial for safeguarding your inner peace.

How to Practice: Start by identifying areas in your life where you feel overextended or drained. Are you saying yes to every request at work? Are you constantly available to friends and family, even when you need downtime? Once you've identified these areas, practice saying *"no"* or *"not right now"* when requests don't align with your priorities.

Practical Insight: When setting boundaries, communicate clearly and kindly. For example, if you need time to recharge after work, let your family know that you'll be taking 30 minutes for yourself before engaging in household activities. By expressing your needs, you create an environment where your inner peace is respected and valued.

Why It Works: Setting boundaries isn't about shutting others out; it's about creating space for what truly matters to you. By protecting your time and energy, you prevent burnout and maintain the mental space needed to cultivate and sustain your inner peace.

Additional Practices for Cultivating Inner Peace

- **Engage in Regular Physical Activity:** Movement is a powerful way to release tension and connect with your body, which in turn fosters inner peace. Whether it's yoga, running, dancing, or a simple walk, find a form of exercise that feels good to you and incorporate it into your routine.

- **Create a Peaceful Environment:** Your surroundings have a significant impact on your state of mind. Take time to declutter your space, add elements of nature (such as plants or natural light), and create a calming atmosphere that supports your sense of peace.

- **Limit Exposure to Negative Influences:** Be mindful of what you consume—whether it's news, social media, or the energy of people around you. Reducing exposure to negativity can help preserve your inner peace and create space for more positive and uplifting influences.

Cultivating Inner Peace as a Lifelong Journey

Remember, cultivating inner peace is not about achieving a perfect state of calm or eliminating all stress from your life. It's about developing the tools and practices that allow you to navigate life's challenges with greater ease, resilience, and clarity. By incorporating these practices into your daily routine, you gradually build a foundation of inner peace that supports you in all aspects of your journey—enabling you to pursue your goals, connect with others, and live more authentically from a place of calm and centeredness.

Action Step: Starting Your Inner Peace Journey

To begin your journey toward inner peace, try incorporating these foundational practices into your daily routine. These steps are designed to help you build awareness, regulate your emotions, and strengthen your resilience:

1. **Five-Minute Mindfulness Practice:** Find a quiet space where you won't be interrupted. Set a timer for five minutes. Close your eyes and focus on your breath. Inhale deeply, and exhale slowly. As thoughts arise, notice them without judgment and gently return your

focus to your breath. This practice cultivates presence and awareness, the foundation of mindfulness and emotional regulation. As you become more comfortable, gradually increase the time spent in this practice.

2. **Emotional Check-In:** Set an alarm or reminder on your phone to check in with yourself at least twice daily. When the reminder goes off, pause and ask yourself, *"How am I feeling right now?"* Identify and label your emotions without judgment. If you notice tension or stress, take three deep breaths, allowing yourself to process the emotion before moving forward. This practice helps you become more aware of your emotional state and strengthens your ability to regulate your responses. Remember to ask yourself, *"What do I need right now?"* when facing negative emotions.

3. **Daily Gratitude Journal:** At the end of the day, spend five minutes journaling about three things you're grateful for, along with one moment where you felt most at peace and one where you felt stressed. Reflect on how you handled both situations. What can you learn from these experiences? How could you bring more awareness, calm, or resilience to similar situations in the future? This practice shifts your focus toward abundance and helps you identify patterns contributing to or detracting from your inner peace.

4. **Mindful Boundary Setting:** Identify one area in your life where you feel overextended or stressed. Set a clear boundary for yourself—whether it's saying no to an additional task at work, carving out time for self-care, or limiting exposure to negative

influences. As you implement this boundary, observe how it impacts your sense of calm and well-being. This practice reinforces the importance of protecting your energy and prioritizing what truly matters.

Ethan in Action: The Power of a Pause

As Ethan sat at his desk, his eyes locked on an email filled with harsh criticism about a recent project he led. *The words stung, and his immediate reaction was to defend himself, to respond with a lengthy explanation to prove his worth. His heart raced, and he could feel the familiar tension rising in his chest—the kind of tension that had always propelled him into overdrive, striving to protect his reputation and avoid failure. In the past, Ethan would have stayed up all night drafting a response, replaying the criticism in his mind and letting it fuel his anxiety.*

But today, something was different. Ethan paused, remembering his recent commitment to cultivating inner peace. He recognized the wave of emotions crashing over him—anger, embarrassment, and self-doubt—and instead of letting them take control, he consciously chose to regulate them. He closed his eyes, took a deep breath, and allowed himself a moment of stillness, engaging in an emotional check-in: ***"What am I feeling right now, and why?"*** *By acknowledging his emotions, he was able to prevent them from dictating his response.*

Next, Ethan opened his mindfulness app and spent five minutes in meditation, focusing on his breath and letting go of the urge to react impulsively. As he practiced this mindfulness, he noticed the tension in his shoulders easing and the sense of urgency fading. He began to view the criticism from a different perspective—not as a personal attack, but as an opportunity for growth and improvement. This shift in awareness reminded him of the third pillar of inner peace: seeing challenges as chances to build resilience.

Empowered by this newfound clarity, Ethan approached the email with a sense of calm and intention. Instead of defending himself, he thoughtfully thanked his colleague for the feedback and expressed a genuine desire to learn and improve. This response, rooted in emotional regulation, mindfulness, and resilience, not only diffused the tension but also led to a more constructive dialogue. His colleague responded positively, appreciating Ethan's willingness to listen and adapt.

By applying his understanding of inner peace, Ethan experienced a breakthrough—realizing that challenges didn't have to disrupt his inner calm but could serve as stepping stones toward growth. This moment reinforced his belief that true strength comes not from reacting defensively, but from responding thoughtfully and with grace, even in the face of discomfort. As Ethan continued his journey, he began to see how inner peace wasn't just a concept but a practical tool that enriched his relationships, enhanced his leadership, and allowed him to navigate life's challenges with greater ease and purpose.

Summary: Defining Inner Peace

In this chapter, we explored the true meaning of inner peace, dismantling common misconceptions and revealing its significance in achieving sustainable success. Unlike the widely held belief that inner peace is a state of constant calmness or detachment from ambition, the chapter clarifies that it is an ongoing journey—a dynamic process of emotional regulation, mindfulness, and resilience that equips individuals to face life's challenges with balance and grace.

Key Takeaways

- Inner peace is an active journey, not a passive state, and it's foundational for achieving true, lasting success.

- The three pillars of inner peace—emotional regulation, mindfulness, and resilience—are essential for navigating life's challenges.

- Success isn't about constant productivity; it's about balancing ambition with inner calm, allowing for a more intentional and fulfilling path.

Conclusion: Inner Peace as the Foundation for Everything

Inner peace is not just a personal luxury; it is a necessity for long-term success and fulfillment. It's the anchor that keeps you grounded amidst life's chaos and the compass that guides you toward a life that is both ambitious and deeply satisfying. By fostering inner peace, you cultivate a state of clarity and resilience that empowers you to navigate challenges with grace, avoid burnout, and stay true to what truly matters.

Without this foundation, the pursuit of success can become an exhausting chase, leaving you feeling unfulfilled and disconnected from your true self. But when you integrate inner peace into your journey, you create the conditions for a more authentic and sustainable path to achievement—one that allows you to thrive, not just survive.

As we move forward, you'll discover that inner peace is not an obstacle to ambition but a powerful ally. It sharpens your focus, enhances creativity, and strengthens resilience, allowing you to pursue your goals with clarity and purpose. But as we navigate the path to success, there's often a hidden challenge that arises—the doubt and insecurity that can undermine even the most peaceful mindset. In the next chapter, we'll explore the shadow of imposter syndrome, a common experience for those striving for greatness, and how embracing both peace and confidence can dismantle self-doubt, enabling you to move forward with genuine self-assurance. Together, let's uncover how balancing ambition with self-acceptance leads to not just success, but a deeper, more authentic sense of achievement.

Three

◊

Letting Go of the Imposter Within

Ethan sat in his office, staring at the email congratulating him on his latest promotion. *His colleagues had already celebrated, and his boss had praised him for his hard work and leadership. From the outside, everything looked perfect—another step up the corporate ladder, more responsibility, more recognition. But inside, Ethan felt a gnawing sense of unease.*

Why me? he thought, the familiar wave of doubt creeping in. What if they realize I don't deserve this?

It wasn't the first time he had felt this way. Despite years of accomplishments and steady growth, Ethan had always carried a secret fear—that he was a fraud. Every success seemed like luck, every praise felt unearned. And now, with more eyes on him than ever before, the pressure to prove himself was overwhelming. He worried that at any moment, someone would call him out, expose him as the imposter he believed himself to be.

The emails continued to flood in—requests for meetings, new projects to oversee, congratulatory messages from team members. But each notification only added to the weight in his chest. He had been playing this role for years—juggling the façade of confidence with the internal chaos of self-doubt—and now it was catching up to him.

Later that evening, Ethan sat at home, reviewing the details of his new position. He could feel the exhaustion setting in, not just from the workload, but from the mental battle he fought each day. How long could he keep this up? The fear of being "found out" lurked behind every decision, every interaction, every task. It wasn't about the work— he knew he could handle that—but the constant pressure to prove that he belonged.

He thought back to a conversation he'd had with his colleague, Rachel, months earlier. She had mentioned something called imposter syndrome—the feeling of being undeserving despite evidence of success. At the time, Ethan had brushed it off. That's for people who aren't really competent, he had thought. But now, as he sat with his doubt, Rachel's words came back to him with a new meaning.

Ethan realized that his achievements, no matter how significant, had never been enough to quiet the voice inside telling him he wasn't worthy. He was constantly chasing the next validation, hoping it would finally silence his doubts. But each milestone only seemed to fuel the fear.

That night, Ethan made a decision. He was tired of living in the shadow of self-doubt, tired of feeling like a fraud in his own life. It was time to confront the fear head-on. He began researching imposter syndrome, reading stories of others who had experienced the same internal struggle. For the first time, he realized he wasn't alone. This wasn't just his battle—it was something many high-achievers faced, and more importantly, something he could overcome.

As Ethan delved deeper, he started to see the pattern. His worth wasn't tied to his next promotion, his next accolade, or the approval of others. It was something intrinsic, something that couldn't be taken away by a mistake or a criticism. Slowly, he began to shift his perspective—away from needing to prove himself and toward accepting that he had already earned his place.

The path ahead wouldn't be easy, but Ethan was ready to walk it. He had spent too many years trying to outrun his fear, but now, he was determined to face it—and to let go of the imposter within.

Introduction: The Internal Saboteur

You've just achieved something big—maybe a promotion, maybe recognition from your peers. On the surface, it should feel like a victory. But instead of the satisfaction you were expecting, a small, insistent voice creeps in: *Do you really deserve this?*

That voice—the internal saboteur—questions everything. It reminds you of every time you felt unprepared, every mistake you've ever made, every moment when things could have gone wrong. It tells you that your success is a fluke, that your achievements aren't truly yours, and that soon, everyone around you will figure out the truth: You don't belong here.

This is the reality of imposter syndrome, a hidden struggle many high achievers face despite outward success. It's the persistent fear of being exposed as a fraud, regardless of the accolades, promotions, or praise you've earned. Even when people tell you how talented or accomplished you are, imposter syndrome convinces you that you've fooled them—that you're not really worthy of their admiration.

Imposter syndrome doesn't discriminate. It affects people across industries and at all stages of their careers—whether they're just starting out or have reached the top of their field. Entrepreneurs, executives, artists, and students can fall under its grip. Some of the most successful individuals, from world leaders to award-winning performers, have admitted to feeling like imposters at times.

But why does this happen? Why do so many talented, capable people struggle to believe in their own abilities?

One reason is that we live in a culture that prizes perfection and constant achievement. Hustle culture feeds into this by equating worth with productivity, and success with external validation. We've been taught that we must continually prove ourselves to be valued. The more we achieve, the more pressure we feel to maintain an image of perfection. This constant need for validation can create a disconnect between how others see us and how we see ourselves. And that gap is where the internal saboteur thrives.

Perfectionism, comparison, and fear of failure all fuel imposter syndrome. You may find yourself setting impossibly high standards, feeling as though anything less than perfection will expose you as a fraud. Or maybe you constantly compare yourself to others, believing that everyone else is more competent or deserving. The fear of being "found out" often leads to overworking, anxiety, and burnout, as you push yourself harder and harder to prove your worth.

But here's the truth: imposter syndrome is not a reflection of your abilities—it's a reflection of your inner dialogue. It's the story you tell yourself, one that often doesn't align with reality. And if left unchecked, this narrative can rob you of your peace, your confidence, and your ability to enjoy your success fully.

In this chapter, we'll explore what imposter syndrome really is, why it manifests in high achievers, and most importantly, how to overcome it. By learning to challenge these feelings of inadequacy and reframe your self-perception, you can silence the internal saboteur and begin to own your success with confidence.

Because the truth is, you've earned your place. You are not an imposter. It's time to stop listening to that voice and start embracing your worth.

What is Imposter Syndrome?

Imposter syndrome is a psychological pattern where individuals doubt their accomplishments and have a persistent fear of being exposed as a "fraud," despite evidence of their competence. Coined in the late 1970s by psychologists Pauline Clance and Suzanne Imes, imposter syndrome is characterized by a belief that any success is due to luck, timing, or external factors—anything but one's own abilities. Those experiencing it often feel as though they've somehow deceived others into believing they are more capable than they truly are, and that it's only a matter of time before they are "found out."[25]

The Symptoms

People suffering from imposter syndrome often exhibit several recognizable symptoms, including:

- Fear of Being "Found Out": A constant fear that others will soon discover they are not as competent as they seem. This can create anxiety around performance reviews, presentations, or any situation where their skills might be assessed.

- Attributing Success to Luck: Even when receiving praise or achieving something significant, individuals with imposter syndrome tend to believe their success is due to luck, timing, or external circumstances rather than their own skills or efforts.

- Downplaying Achievements: They may brush off compliments or recognition, minimizing their accomplishments as though they weren't significant or that "anyone" could have done it.

- Perfectionism and Overworking: To avoid being exposed, people often overwork or strive for unattainable perfection, believing they need to go above and beyond to prove they belong.

Despite their achievements, those with imposter syndrome feel they haven't truly earned their success, and this cognitive dissonance creates immense internal stress.

Connection to Hustle Culture

In today's hustle culture, perceived marks of success—titles, wealth, and relentless productivity—create the perfect environment for imposter syndrome to thrive. This culture emphasizes the idea that self-worth is tied to constant achievement, often equating being "busy" with being successful. In this environment, people who already doubt their abilities feel even more pressure to meet impossible standards.

When success is framed in this way, the focus shifts from *being* to *doing*. You aren't worthy because of who you are, but because of what you produce. This can feed the imposter syndrome cycle—people push themselves harder, seeking validation through work, and even when they achieve milestones, it rarely feels like enough. They continue to doubt whether they truly deserve their success, which drives them to hustle even more, perpetuating a loop of anxiety and self-doubt.

Hustle culture, with its constant drive for more—more hours, more output, more achievements—leaves little room for self-reflection or self-compassion. It glorifies overworking and pushes individuals to focus on external benchmarks like salary, recognition, or position. When these external measures become the only way to assess success, people who suffer from imposter syndrome feel an overwhelming need to prove themselves, fueling anxiety, burnout, and the belief that they are undeserving.

Who Experiences It?

Imposter syndrome is not exclusive to certain types of people—it can affect anyone, regardless of their level of success or skill. In fact, it's often the most accomplished individuals who feel this the most intensely. High achievers, in particular, may struggle because their internal expectations of perfection clash with the reality that even successful people make mistakes or have limitations.

This syndrome is so widespread that even some of the world's most prominent figures have admitted to experiencing it.

For example, Michelle Obama, former First Lady of the United States, has spoken openly about her struggles with imposter syndrome, even while attending Princeton and Harvard, and later as she stepped into the global spotlight. Despite her achievements, she confessed to feeling like she didn't deserve to be there.[26]

Tom Hanks, one of the most well-regarded actors of his generation, has admitted that he still sometimes feels like an imposter, wondering when people will "realize" he's not as talented as they think.[27]

By sharing their experiences, these public figures remind us that imposter syndrome doesn't disappear with more success. In fact, the pressure to maintain a certain level of achievement can exacerbate it. The more successful you are, the higher the stakes feel, and the more you may believe that at some point, you'll be "found out."

Understanding that imposter syndrome is common—particularly among people who have worked hard and achieved significant success—helps to normalize the experience. You're not alone if you've felt this way, and it doesn't mean there's anything wrong with you. In fact, feeling like an imposter can be a sign that you're pushing yourself out of your comfort zone and growing in ways that challenge old beliefs about what you're capable of.

By acknowledging imposter syndrome as a widespread experience, especially in environments driven by constant achievement, we can begin to dismantle its power. Understanding that even those at the highest levels feel these doubts is the first step in reframing how we approach our own success. In the next section, we'll examine how imposter syndrome disrupts inner peace.

The Impact of Imposter Syndrome on Inner Peace

Imposter syndrome does more than shake your confidence—it creates a powerful internal struggle that undermines your sense of peace. The weight of constantly feeling unworthy takes a toll on both your mental and emotional well-being, creating ripples that disrupt every corner of your life. Let's explore how this manifests in two key ways:

Emotional Toll

Imposter syndrome generates a continuous stream of self-doubt and anxiety, leaving you in a constant state of emotional unrest. You may find yourself questioning your achievements, wondering if you've somehow deceived others into thinking you're more capable than you feel. This fear of being "found out" drives you to work harder, not out of passion or purpose, but out of a deep-seated need to prove you belong. The endless pressure leads to a lack of fulfillment, even as you meet goals. Rather than feeling pride in your success, you feel a growing sense of unease, as if each milestone raises the stakes of being exposed. The result is a relentless emotional drain, robbing you of moments of joy and personal peace.

Perfectionism and Burnout

A common response to imposter syndrome is to overcompensate through perfectionism. The fear of making mistakes or being seen as inadequate can push you to work tirelessly, aiming for flawless results in every task. You may find yourself constantly pushing boundaries, believing that any slip-up will confirm your deepest fears of not being good enough. This pursuit of perfection, however, is unsustainable. It often leads to burnout, as the effort to maintain this facade becomes exhausting. Burnout not only impacts your productivity but also further reinforces feelings of inadequacy, fueling the cycle of self-doubt. The more you strive for perfection, the more distant inner peace becomes, as the constant overworking leaves you physically and emotionally drained.

Imposter syndrome not only disrupts emotional well-being through anxiety and fear but also creates a destructive cycle of perfectionism and burnout. These impacts make it difficult to cultivate the sense of inner peace we seek. Recognizing and addressing this internal struggle is essential for reclaiming your emotional balance and shifting from self-doubt to self-acceptance. In the next section, we'll explore strategies for overcoming these feelings and finding greater peace within yourself.

Building Confidence Through Self-Acceptance

Imposter syndrome thrives when we fail to accept and recognize our strengths. Building confidence is about embracing who you are— strengths and weaknesses alike. Self-acceptance is a key step in dismantling the insecurities that feed imposter syndrome, shifting the focus from external validation to an internal sense of worth.

Understanding Your Strengths

Imposter syndrome often blinds us to our real talents and accomplishments, leaving us feeling as though we've simply "gotten lucky" or don't truly deserve our success. To build genuine confidence, it's essential to reconnect with your unique strengths. Start by creating a list of achievements you're proud of, no matter how small. These could be work-related, personal victories, or times when you've helped others. Reflect on the skills or qualities that led you to those moments, reinforcing the fact that your success is a direct result of your efforts, not chance.

Practical Insight: Recognizing your strengths isn't about inflating your ego—it's about seeing yourself clearly. When you acknowledge your abilities, you're better equipped to push back against the doubts that arise when imposter syndrome strikes.

Shifting Focus from Approval to Authenticity

Much of imposter syndrome is rooted in a desire for external validation. We worry about whether others see us as capable or competent, constantly striving for approval. But lasting confidence comes from shifting that focus inward—toward authenticity. Ask yourself: *Am I living in a way that aligns with my values and true self?* When you base your sense of success on how authentically you show up in the world, the pressure to "prove" yourself to others fades.

Practical Insight: Begin each day by checking in with yourself: Are your actions aligned with your core values? Are you doing work or engaging in relationships that feel meaningful? When your confidence is built on authenticity, imposter syndrome loses its power to control how you see yourself.

Balancing Confidence with Humility

Self-acceptance isn't about pretending you're perfect—it's about being at peace with who you are, including both your strengths and areas for growth. Imposter syndrome often tricks us into thinking we need to be perfect to deserve our achievements. But in reality, true confidence comes from embracing both the things you excel at and the things you're still learning.

Balancing confidence with humility allows you to grow without the fear of being "exposed" as an imposter. Confidence means recognizing your value; humility means understanding that you're always evolving. By accepting that no one has to be flawless, you free yourself from the fear of failure and cultivate lasting inner peace.

By building confidence through self-acceptance, you create a strong foundation to combat imposter syndrome. Understanding your strengths, shifting your focus from external approval to living authentically, and balancing confidence with humility help diminish feelings of inadequacy. These mindset shifts allow you to approach life with greater peace and resilience.

Imposter syndrome not only disrupts your confidence but also undermines your sense of inner peace, creating a cycle of anxiety, perfectionism, and burnout. To break this cycle, it's essential to shift your focus inward and adopt strategies that build resilience and self-acceptance. By incorporating intentional practices into your daily routine, you can gradually quiet the voice of doubt, reclaim your peace, and restore a healthier sense of self-worth. In the next section, we'll explore practical steps to help you overcome imposter syndrome and strengthen your inner confidence.

Practical Strategies for Overcoming Imposter Syndrome

Overcoming imposter syndrome is not about eliminating self-doubt altogether, but about learning how to manage and challenge it. Imposter syndrome convinces us that no matter how much we achieve, it's never quite enough—that we've somehow tricked others into believing we belong. This mindset can be deeply disruptive, eroding confidence and preventing us from finding peace in our accomplishments. However, through intentional practices, we can begin to shift this narrative. By reframing our thoughts, celebrating successes, and seeking support, we reclaim our sense of worth and begin to quiet the inner critic.

Reframing Negative Thoughts

Imposter syndrome thrives on negative self-talk—those internalized beliefs that tell you you're not good enough. The process of reframing these thoughts involves identifying when they occur and consciously challenging them. Start by acknowledging the thought, such as, *I'm not qualified for this*, and then ask yourself, *What is the evidence for this belief?* More often than not, you'll find that the thought is rooted in fear rather than fact. Creating a "thought log" is a powerful way to track these moments of doubt and rewrite them. Document the negative thought, then counter it with a truth: *I've earned my place by developing valuable skills*. With time, you'll begin to see that these moments of insecurity don't define your worth or abilities.

Reframing is a practice that requires patience and consistency. It doesn't mean ignoring or suppressing doubts but rather teaching yourself to respond to them with greater self-compassion and realism. Over time, these small shifts in thinking accumulate, helping you build resilience against the voice of imposter syndrome.

Celebrate Successes

One of the most damaging effects of imposter syndrome is that it keeps you from acknowledging your accomplishments. No matter how much you achieve, it's easy to downplay success and focus on what you haven't yet done. To break this habit, develop a ritual of celebrating your wins—big or small. Create a "wins journal" where you regularly document achievements, whether it's finishing a project, receiving positive feedback, or even taking a small step toward a larger goal. This practice serves as a tangible reminder that you are making progress, and it counters the narrative that you are "not enough."

In moments of self-doubt, revisit your wins journal. It's easy to forget how much you've accomplished when you're caught in the cycle of negative thinking. Seeing your success on paper reinforces that you've earned your place through hard work and dedication. Celebrating even small victories helps ground you in the present, reminding you that progress is ongoing and worthy of recognition.

Stop Comparing

Imposter syndrome often worsens when we compare ourselves to others. Whether it's a colleague who seems to excel effortlessly or the carefully curated lives we see on social media, these comparisons can fuel feelings of inadequacy. The truth is, comparison rarely gives you a full picture of someone else's struggles or challenges, and it distorts how you see your own path.

One of the most effective ways to stop comparing is to limit exposure to environments that trigger it. If social media makes you feel less-than, take regular breaks and focus on your own growth. Practice mindfulness by centering your attention on what you have accomplished and the progress you are making, rather than looking outward for validation. Mindfulness exercises like journaling or meditation can help you stay rooted in your personal journey, reducing the urge to measure yourself against others.

Seek Support

Imposter syndrome thrives in isolation. The more you keep your feelings of doubt to yourself, the more power they seem to hold. Sharing these thoughts with trusted friends, mentors, or even a therapist can break that cycle. When you talk openly about your struggles, you'll often find that others have experienced the same thing. Imposter syndrome is far more common than it seems, especially among high achievers.

Talking to someone who knows you well can provide much-needed perspective. They can remind you of your strengths and reflect on the accomplishments you may overlook. In professional settings, a mentor can be especially valuable, offering guidance and reassurance when self-doubt arises. Seeking support is not a sign of weakness—it's a way to gain clarity and reduce the emotional burden that imposter syndrome imposes. It can help you realize that you don't have to navigate these feelings alone.

Action Steps: Overcoming Imposter Syndrome

To combat imposter syndrome and build a more resilient sense of confidence, incorporate these practices into your daily routine. These steps are designed to help you challenge self-doubt, celebrate achievements, and nurture self-acceptance:

1. **Thought Log Reframing:** Start a thought log where you write down negative self-talk each time it arises. Review the thought and ask, What's the evidence for this belief? Then, replace it with a positive truth, such as, I earned this through my skills and hard work. This practice helps retrain your mind to respond with self-compassion rather than doubt.

2. **Daily Wins Journal:** End each day by writing down three achievements—whether big or small. These could be completing a task, receiving positive feedback, or learning something new. Reflect on how each win contributes to your growth. In moments of self-doubt, revisit this journal to remind yourself of your progress and successes, reinforcing your self-worth.

3. **Limiting Comparison:** Limit exposure to triggers of comparison, like social media or competitive work environments. Practice mindfulness by focusing on your own growth and progress instead of external achievements. When you feel tempted to compare, pause and ask, Am I measuring my worth by someone else's success or my own? Recenter yourself on what truly matters to you.

Ethan in Action: Letting Go of the Imposter Within

Months after that sleepless night of self-doubt, Ethan found himself once again at a pivotal moment. He had been invited to present at an industry conference—something he'd always considered a career milestone. The invitation was proof that his work was respected, that he was seen as a leader in his field. Yet, as the event drew nearer, the familiar shadow of imposter syndrome crept back in.

He stood backstage, rehearsing his speech for the hundredth time, feeling the weight of his doubts pressing down on him. What if they don't take me seriously? What if I stumble? What if they realize I'm not as competent as they think? His mind swirled with a thousand versions of failure.

But this time, something was different. Ethan paused, taking a deep breath, and reminded himself of the tools he had been practicing over the past few months. He had made a commitment to stop letting these doubts define him, to break free from the endless cycle of seeking validation. The imposter syndrome that had once paralyzed him no longer had the same hold.

Instead of pushing the doubts away, Ethan acknowledged them. He could feel the fear bubbling up inside, but now he had the awareness to deal with it. He remembered what he had learned: the feeling of being an imposter didn't reflect his reality. It was a mental trap—one that countless others had fallen into, but one that didn't have to dictate his behavior.

He quietly stepped aside from the backstage chaos and opened his notebook. In it, he had written a list of his achievements—not to boast, but to remind himself of the concrete evidence that he belonged here. As he read through the list, he felt a shift in his mindset. These were not just lucky breaks or moments of chance. They were the result of years of hard work, perseverance, and skill. He had earned this.

Next, Ethan went through his self-talk reframing exercise—one he had practiced many times before. When the voice inside whispered, You're going to fail, he countered with, I'm prepared and capable. I've faced challenges like this before and succeeded. The more he replaced his negative thoughts, the more grounded he felt.

He took a final breath, closed the notebook, and looked toward the stage. He knew the doubts wouldn't disappear completely. They might always be there, lingering at the edges of his mind. But now, they no longer controlled him. He was learning to coexist with them, using them as fuel to stay grounded and focused rather than letting them spiral into self-sabotage.

As he walked onto the stage and saw the crowd of expectant faces, the familiar flicker of anxiety sparked—but Ethan had tools to manage it now. He began his presentation with confidence, focusing on his message rather than on whether people believed in him. He no longer needed external validation to feel worthy. He had given that to himself.

After the event, Ethan reflected on the experience. Had it been perfect? No. He had stumbled on a word or two, and there were a few moments where his nerves had flared. But none of that mattered. What mattered was that he had shown up fully, owning his role and his accomplishments without shrinking back in fear. He no longer felt like an imposter. He felt like a leader—one who could rise above doubt and continue growing, no matter what challenges lay ahead.

This was the breakthrough Ethan had been seeking all along. Letting go of the need to prove himself didn't diminish his ambition or drive. It freed him to pursue success from a place of calm and confidence, knowing that he belonged exactly where he was.

Summary: Letting Go of the Imposter Within

Imposter syndrome can quietly undermine both your confidence and inner peace, leaving you feeling like you don't belong, despite your accomplishments. This chapter revealed the roots of imposter syndrome and how it's fueled by perfectionism, comparison, and external validation.

Key Takeaways

- Reframe Negative Thoughts: Challenge self-doubt and reframe it with evidence of your competence.

- Celebrate Wins: Recognize and document your achievements.

- Limit Comparison: Focus on your personal growth.

- Seek Support: Reach out to mentors or trusted allies to gain perspective.

Conclusion: Breaking the Grip of Imposter Syndrome

Imposter syndrome may persist, but it doesn't have to control your story. By reframing negative thoughts, celebrating your accomplishments, and seeking support, you can loosen its grip and embrace self-acceptance. As we've explored in this chapter, redefining your idea of success is a key part of overcoming imposter syndrome—shifting the focus from external validation to inner worth.

Now is the time to challenge your inner saboteur, silence the voice that questions your worth, and embrace the truth of what you've earned. You've already put in the work and achieved success—now, it's about fully recognizing that you deserve to be where you are. Let go of the doubts that have held you back and step confidently into the space you've rightfully claimed.

As we move into the next chapter, we'll explore the delicate balance between success and inner peace, and how redefining success can create a more fulfilling, peaceful path forward.

Four

∽❦∼

The Interplay Between Success and Peace

As Ethan approached a major project deadline, the weight of his packed calendar pressed down on him. Meetings, tasks, client calls—it was all too familiar, the kind of pressure that had once pushed him into overdrive. In the past, Ethan would have worked late into the night, fueled by the belief that hustle was the only path to success. But this time, things were different.

Ethan had made a commitment to himself, one rooted in the lessons he had begun to embrace: success didn't have to come at the cost of his well-being. With this in mind, he paused, taking a moment to center himself before diving into his work. He opened his journal and asked, **"What would it look like to succeed today without losing my sense of peace?"**

That simple question marked the start of a shift. As the day unfolded, Ethan faced a critical decision: an email from his boss offered the

81

chance to lead a high-profile campaign. The opportunity was tempting—the kind of project that could propel his career forward. But something held him back. Could he take on such a demanding role without sacrificing the inner balance he was working to cultivate?

Instead of rushing into the decision, Ethan took time to reflect. He asked himself not what this project could give him, but what it might cost. In the past, he would have pushed through without hesitation. Now, however, he proposed a compromise—clear boundaries to protect his time and energy. To his surprise, his boss was not only understanding but supportive.

As Ethan continued this journey, his approach to both life and work began to evolve. A conversation with a colleague, Rachel, further solidified his belief that success didn't have to mean sacrifice. "It's not just about what you achieve," she had said. "It's about how you feel along the way." Inspired by Rachel's words, Ethan began practicing mindfulness more intentionally, bringing greater awareness to each moment and each interaction.

During tense meetings, Ethan chose to listen before reacting, observing not only his colleagues' words but their emotions. The shift in his approach did not go unnoticed. "You're really listening," a teammate commented one day after a meeting where Ethan's calm input had helped the team reach a consensus.

But this journey was not without setbacks. Criticism from a client triggered old habits of self-doubt and the urge to overwork, but Ethan caught himself. Instead of reacting, he paused, took a walk, and reframed the challenge as an opportunity for growth. This simple shift— responding from a place of curiosity instead of defensiveness—helped turn a potential failure into a moment of progress and trust.

Looking back, Ethan realized that his relationship with success had fundamentally changed. He was still ambitious, still driven, but now his success was rooted in how he navigated the process, not just in the outcomes. The once-conflicting ideas of peace and ambition had become two sides of the same coin.

His story, though still unfolding, revealed a truth he had resisted for so long: real success was not just about what he achieved, but about who he became along the way. This realization was about to guide him into the next chapter of his journey, where he would explore the dynamic interplay between success and peace.

Introduction: Peace and Ambition Can Coexist

For years, society has ingrained in us the belief that success demands constant effort, sacrifice, and unyielding ambition. We hear stories of entrepreneurs pulling all-nighters, executives sacrificing weekends, and athletes pushing their bodies to the brink, all in the name of achievement. It's no wonder we've come to equate success with relentless hustle, convinced that slowing down means falling behind. Yet, despite all the striving, many who reach the pinnacle of their careers often find themselves feeling burned out, unfulfilled, and disconnected from their true selves.

But what if we've been looking at success all wrong? What if the relentless chase isn't the key to greatness but rather the very thing holding us back? What if, instead of losing ourselves in the pursuit, we could find a way to bring our whole selves into the journey?

In this chapter, we'll challenge the idea that ambition and inner peace are at odds. Through exploring how these two forces can coexist harmoniously, we'll uncover why inner peace isn't a sign of weakness or a luxury reserved for the leisurely—it's a powerful tool that can elevate our performance, resilience, and creativity. Consider some of the most influential and successful individuals in the world. Many, from Steve Jobs to Oprah Winfrey, have openly credited practices like meditation, mindfulness, and introspection as essential to their success. These practices didn't hinder their achievements; they enhanced them.

Imagine a life where you wake up excited about your goals, but instead of feeling overwhelmed, you feel grounded, focused, and aligned with your values. Picture tackling challenges with clarity and grace, making decisions from a place of confidence rather than fear or urgency. This is the power of integrating inner peace with ambition.

By the end of this chapter, you'll see that cultivating inner peace isn't just a way to survive the pressures of life—it's a path to thriving in your personal and professional pursuits. When you learn to approach your ambitions from a place of calm and clarity, you don't just achieve more; you achieve in a way that honors who you are. You'll find that true success isn't about how much you can do but about how intentionally and joyfully you can do it.

The False Dichotomy: Peace vs. Success

For much of modern history, peace and success have been viewed as opposites, as though one must be sacrificed for the other. Success is often associated with relentless action, achievement, and forward momentum, while peace is equated with stillness, passivity, or even a lack of ambition. The prevailing belief is that to reach the top, you must push yourself to the limit, sacrificing rest and tranquility along the way. But this is a false dichotomy that traps us in a never-ending cycle of striving without fulfillment.

In reality, peace and success are not mutually exclusive; they can, and often do, enhance one another. Inner peace doesn't require abandoning your goals or ambitions; it empowers you to pursue them with greater clarity, focus, and resilience. When you cultivate inner peace, you create the mental space needed for more thoughtful decision-making, increased creativity, and sustained energy, which are all essential ingredients for long-term success.

Consider how peace plays a role in some of the most demanding professions:

- **High-Performing Athletes:** Many elite athletes, from LeBron James to Novak Djokovic, attribute their success to mindfulness and mental relaxation techniques. Before stepping onto the court or field, they take time to center themselves, breathing deeply, visualizing success, and clearing their minds of distractions. This mental preparation allows them to stay calm under pressure, adapt to unexpected challenges, and perform at their highest level.[28]

- **Business Leaders and Innovators:** Some of the world's most successful business leaders, such as Jeff Weiner, the former CEO of LinkedIn, and Marc Benioff, the CEO of Salesforce, have embraced mindfulness as a core component of their leadership. Weiner begins his day with a meditation practice, while Benioff schedules "mindfulness breaks" throughout his busy schedule. Both have spoken about how these practices help them make clearer decisions, stay connected with their vision, and lead with empathy. By integrating inner peace into their routines, they can navigate the high-stakes, fast-paced world of business without being overwhelmed.[29]

- **Creatives and Artists:** Renowned creatives like Lady Gaga and Elizabeth Gilbert have indeed spoken about how inner peace and mindfulness are integral to their creative process. Elizabeth Gilbert, author of *Eat, Pray, Love*, has shared how meditation allows her to tap into a deeper sense of creativity, creating from a place of joy rather than fear. For Gilbert, mindfulness isn't just a tool for calm—it's a way to nurture her creative well, enabling her to approach her work with authenticity and presence.[30] Similarly, Lady Gaga incorporates daily meditation into her routine to stay grounded amid the pressures of fame. She has mentioned that meditation helps her maintain balance and manage the intense emotions that come with her high-energy performances and public persona.[31]

Why the False Dichotomy Exists

The idea that peace and success are incompatible often stems from societal norms and conditioning. From a young age, many of us are taught that achievement requires constant effort and that rest is a sign of laziness or lack of ambition. In school, we're rewarded for working hard, pulling all-nighters, and pushing ourselves beyond our limits. As we enter the workforce, the culture of hustle becomes even more pronounced, with late nights, packed schedules, and the glorification of being "busy" becoming badges of honor.

This mindset creates a narrow definition of success—one that is measured solely by external achievements, titles, and material gains. In contrast, inner peace is often dismissed as something that can wait until retirement, vacation, or some far-off point when we've "earned" the right to relax. But what if we didn't have to wait? What if peace could be part of the journey, not just the destination?

How Peace Enhances Success

Inner peace provides the foundation from which sustainable, meaningful success can grow. Here's how:

- **Enhanced Decision-Making:** When we're constantly in a state of stress or urgency, we tend to make impulsive or fear-driven decisions. However, when we approach situations from a place of calm, we gain perspective and can assess challenges more clearly. Inner peace creates the mental space needed to evaluate options, consider long-term consequences, and make choices aligned with our values and goals. This leads to more thoughtful, strategic actions that propel us toward true success.

- **Increased Creativity and Innovation:** Stress narrows our focus and inhibits creative thinking, while peace opens up mental pathways that allow ideas to flow freely. When you're not bogged down by anxiety or the pressure to perform, you become more receptive to new possibilities and solutions. This is why many breakthroughs happen during moments of relaxation, such as taking a walk, daydreaming, or even meditating. The brain's most innovative insights often emerge when we're in a state of ease, not when we're forcing them.

- **Greater Resilience and Adaptability:** Success is rarely a straight path; it's filled with setbacks, obstacles, and unexpected turns. When we cultivate inner peace, we develop the resilience needed to navigate these challenges without being derailed. Instead of reacting with panic or frustration, we can respond with clarity, adaptability, and a sense of calm, allowing us to bounce back more quickly and learn from each experience.

Realizing the Truth: Peace and Success as Partners

The truth is, peace and success are not opposing forces—they are partners on the journey toward a fulfilling life. When we redefine success to include not just what we achieve but how we feel and who we become in the process, we unlock a deeper sense of purpose and fulfillment. The most extraordinary accomplishments often come from those who have learned to cultivate a sense of inner calm, allowing them to bring their best selves to every challenge, opportunity, and moment.

Ultimately, the most powerful and enduring successes are born not from endless striving but from a place of balance, where peace fuels ambition, and ambition is guided by peace. As we move forward in this chapter, we will explore practical strategies for integrating these two forces so that you can pursue your goals with clarity, intention, and a profound sense of inner fulfillment.

The Calm Within the Storm: How Inner Peace Fuels Success

Imagine you're sailing a ship through rough seas. The wind is howling, the waves are crashing, and your instinct might be to panic, adjusting the sails frantically with every gust of wind. But an experienced sailor understands that to navigate the storm, they must remain calm and steady, trusting in their skill and judgment. In much the same way, inner peace serves as your anchor amid life's turbulence, providing the clarity and composure needed to navigate challenges without losing direction.

Inner peace is not about avoiding the storms of life but about finding stillness within them. It's what allows you to tap into your inner strength, remain focused under pressure, and adapt to whatever comes your way. Here's how inner peace can actively fuel your success:

Improved Decision-Making

When you're at peace, you're less likely to make impulsive decisions driven by fear, stress, or external pressures. Instead, you create the mental space to step back, assess situations objectively, and make choices that align with your values and long-term goals.

Example: Consider Warren Buffett, one of the most successful investors in history. Buffett is known for his calm and composed approach to decision-making, even during times of market turmoil. He doesn't let panic or external noise influence his investment choices; instead, he evaluates opportunities with a clear, patient mindset. This ability to stay calm in the face of uncertainty has been a key factor in his enduring success.[32]

Scientific Insight: Studies in neuroscience have shown that when we're stressed, our brains enter a "fight-or-flight" mode, which limits our ability to think rationally and creatively. By cultivating inner peace through mindfulness and meditation, we can engage the prefrontal cortex—the part of the brain responsible for logical thinking and decision-making—allowing us to make more thoughtful and effective choices.[33]

Takeaway: The next time you're faced with a tough decision, take a moment to pause, breathe, and reconnect with your inner calm. This simple practice can help you approach challenges with greater clarity and make decisions that align with your true intentions.

Enhanced Focus and Clarity

Inner peace allows you to concentrate on what truly matters, filtering out the noise of stress and anxiety that often distracts us from our priorities. When you're at peace, your mind is less cluttered, enabling you to devote your energy to tasks that have the most significant impact.

Example: Steve Jobs, the co-founder of Apple, was known for his relentless focus and clarity of vision. Jobs attributed much of his ability to concentrate and innovate to his practice of Zen meditation, which helped him cultivate a sense of inner peace. This calmness allowed him to zero in on what mattered most, resulting in groundbreaking products that changed the tech industry forever.[34]

Practical Insight: When you're in a state of inner peace, you're less likely to be pulled in multiple directions by distractions, emails, or social media. This ability to maintain focus helps you produce higher-quality work, complete tasks more efficiently, and make progress toward your goals.

Takeaway: To enhance your focus, start by incorporating short moments of mindfulness into your day. Even taking just five minutes to sit quietly, breathe deeply, and clear your mind can help you regain clarity and approach your work with renewed concentration.

Resilience in the Face of Challenges

Success is rarely a straight path—it's often filled with setbacks, failures, and unexpected obstacles. Inner peace equips you with the resilience needed to bounce back from these challenges without being overwhelmed by frustration or self-doubt. Instead of seeing setbacks as roadblocks, you begin to view them as opportunities for growth and learning.

Example: J.K. Rowling, the author of the Harry Potter series, faced numerous rejections before her manuscript was accepted. Despite experiencing hardships, including financial struggles and personal setbacks, she maintained a sense of inner calm and resilience that allowed her to keep pursuing her dream. Her perseverance, guided by an inner sense of purpose, ultimately led to one of the most successful literary careers in history.[35]

Scientific Insight: Research published in the "Journal of Personality and Psychology" found that individuals who practice mindfulness and maintain inner peace are more likely to exhibit resilience when faced with adversity. They experience lower levels of stress and are better able to regulate their emotions, which enables them to adapt and recover more quickly from setbacks.[36]

Takeaway: When you encounter a challenge, instead of reacting with frustration, try to approach it with curiosity and openness. Ask yourself, *"What can I learn from this?"* By maintaining a sense of inner peace, you can turn obstacles into stepping stones on your path to success.

Creativity and Innovation

Stress and pressure narrow your thinking, often pushing you into a reactive mode where you're focused solely on survival. In contrast, when you're at peace, you open up mental space for creative thinking and problem-solving. Many breakthroughs in business, art, and science occur during moments of stillness or relaxation when the mind is free to explore new possibilities.

Example: Albert Einstein, one of the greatest minds in history, famously said that his best ideas often came to him when he was relaxed or engaged in simple activities like playing the violin. This state of inner peace allowed him to access a deeper level of creativity, leading to insights that revolutionized our understanding of physics.[37]

Scientific Insight: A study published in the journal "Psychological Science" found that individuals who practice mindfulness meditation display increased divergent thinking—a key component of creativity. By quieting the mind and allowing it to wander, you create the conditions for original ideas and innovative solutions to emerge.[38]

Takeaway: Embrace moments of stillness and relaxation as opportunities for inspiration. The next time you feel stuck or need a creative breakthrough, step away from your work, take a walk, meditate, or engage in an activity that brings you joy. You might be surprised by the insights that come to you when your mind is at ease.

Putting It All Together: The Power of Inner Peace in Your Success Journey

When you cultivate inner peace, you unlock the potential to navigate life's storms with greater confidence, resilience, and creativity. This sense of calm becomes your greatest ally, allowing you to steer your ship steadily toward success, no matter how rough the seas may be. By integrating inner peace into your daily routine, you'll find that you're not only more capable of achieving your goals but that you do so with a sense of joy, purpose, and fulfillment.

As you move forward, remember that the goal is not to eliminate stress or challenges but to find your center within them. In this way, you become the sailor who, despite the storm, sails with unwavering focus, clarity, and strength—achieving more than you ever thought possible.

Aligning Success with Your Values

One of the most transformative benefits of integrating inner peace into your pursuit of success is that it helps you stay aligned with your deepest values and aspirations. In today's fast-paced world, it's all too easy to get caught up in chasing external markers of success—whether it's financial wealth, career advancement, or public recognition—only to realize, often too late, that you've lost sight of who you truly are. Many people reach the pinnacle of their careers only to find themselves asking, *"Was it worth sacrificing my relationships, health, or integrity?"*

When you cultivate inner peace, however, you gain the clarity needed to evaluate your goals from a more centered perspective. Instead of being swept away by the expectations of others or societal pressures, you have the mental space to ask yourself, *"Is this truly what I want?"* Inner peace becomes your compass, guiding you toward choices that reflect your authentic self and ensuring that your pursuit of success feels both meaningful and fulfilling.

The Trap of External Success

It's a familiar story: you set out with a dream, and somewhere along the way, you start to measure your worth by promotions, titles, or material possessions. While these achievements may bring temporary satisfaction, they often fail to provide lasting fulfillment. This disconnect happens because external success can never fully compensate for the loss of inner alignment. As you climb higher on the ladder of success, the rungs feel increasingly emptier if they don't lead you closer to what genuinely matters.

Example: Take Howard Schultz, the former CEO of Starbucks, who stepped down from his role at the height of his career. Despite his professional success, Schultz realized he needed to reconnect with his core values of community and social impact. He chose to devote his time to philanthropy and initiatives that aligned with his purpose, demonstrating that true success is not just about building a profitable business but about contributing to something greater than oneself.[39]

How Inner Peace Fosters Value Alignment

When you operate from a place of inner peace, you develop a heightened awareness of what truly matters to you. This sense of calm creates the space needed to reflect on your values, enabling you to make choices that resonate with your authentic self. Here's how inner peace helps you align your success with your values:

Clarity in Decision-Making: Inner peace allows you to slow down and evaluate your options without being swayed by external pressures or the fear of missing out (FOMO). This clarity helps you identify which opportunities align with your core values and which are simply distractions.

Practical Insight: The next time you're faced with a major decision, take a few moments to sit quietly and ask yourself, *"Does this align with my values? Will this decision bring me closer to the life I* *want to create?"* By integrating this practice into your routine, you'll begin to make choices that feel true to who you are.

Staying True Amidst Challenges: In the pursuit of success, it's inevitable that you'll encounter challenges, setbacks, and opportunities that test your integrity. When you're grounded in inner peace, you're more likely to stay true to your principles, even when it's tempting to take shortcuts or compromise your values for short-term gains.

Example: Consider the story of Patagonia's founder, Yvon Chouinard. Despite running a billion-dollar company, Chouinard has consistently prioritized environmental sustainability, even when it meant sacrificing potential profits. By staying true to his values, he not only built a successful brand but also created a legacy that reflects his deep commitment to protecting the planet.[40]

Finding Fulfillment Beyond Achievement: When you align your success with your values, you begin to find fulfillment in the process, not just the outcome. Inner peace helps you appreciate the journey and the growth that comes with it rather than constantly chasing the next goalpost. This shift in perspective transforms success from a destination into a deeply rewarding experience.

Practical Insight: Integrate gratitude into your daily routine by reflecting on moments that align with your values. Celebrate not just the milestones you achieve but the ways you showed up authentically and stayed true to your principles. This practice reinforces the connection between inner peace and value-driven success.

The Profound Sense of Fulfillment

When you operate from a place of inner peace, success takes on a new meaning. It's no longer just about hitting targets, earning accolades, or climbing the next rung of the ladder; it becomes about living in alignment with your purpose and values. This alignment not only creates a more profound sense of fulfillment but also serves as a protective shield against burnout, stress, and the emptiness that often accompanies chasing goals that aren't truly yours.

Imagine reaching the end of a long journey and realizing that every step you took brought you closer to your true self—that the success you achieved wasn't just about external recognition but was a reflection of your deepest values and desires. That's the kind of success that lasts. It's not fleeting or conditional; it's a success that nourishes your soul and enriches your life.

As you continue your journey, remember that inner peace isn't just about finding stillness; it's about finding your true north. By cultivating this peace, you create the conditions to pursue your goals with intention, authenticity, and a sense of joy, knowing that every step you take is a reflection of who you truly are.

The Role of Mindfulness in Success

Mindfulness is more than just a buzzword; it's a transformative practice that helps bridge the gap between inner peace and ambition. By cultivating mindfulness, you gain the ability to approach your work, goals, and daily life with greater awareness, focus, and intentionality. Instead of mindlessly chasing success or getting caught up in the whirlwind of daily pressures, mindfulness invites you to work with purpose and clarity, ensuring that every step you take is aligned with your true self.

Let's explore how mindfulness can be integrated into your journey toward success:

Mindfulness in Daily Decisions

One of the simplest but most powerful ways to incorporate mindfulness into your pursuit of success is by bringing awareness to your daily decisions. In the hustle of everyday life, it's easy to operate on autopilot, making choices based on fear, stress, or external pressures rather than intentionality. However, by taking a moment to pause before making decisions, you create the space to act from a place of alignment with your values and long-term vision.

Example: Consider an entrepreneur facing the decision of whether to take on a new client. In the past, they might have accepted every opportunity out of fear of missing out or because they felt pressured to grow their business rapidly. However, by pausing and reflecting mindfully, they might realize that this particular client's values don't align with their own, or that the additional workload would disrupt their work-life balance. This moment of mindfulness allows them to make a more intentional choice, ensuring their path to success remains in harmony with their well-being.

Practical Insight: Before making a significant decision, practice the "STOP" method:

- Stop what you're doing.

- Take a deep breath.

- Observe your thoughts, feelings, and physical sensations.

- Proceed with intention, making a decision that aligns with your values and goals.

By incorporating this simple practice, you'll start making choices that reflect your true priorities rather than being driven by impulse or external expectations.

Mindful Goal Setting

In a world that often glorifies relentless ambition and the pursuit of externally defined success, it's easy to lose sight of what truly matters to you. Mindful goal setting encourages you to shift your focus from chasing societal benchmarks to pursuing goals that resonate with your personal values and aspirations.

Example: Oprah Winfrey, one of the most successful media moguls in the world, attributes much of her success to setting goals that align with her purpose and values. Instead of focusing solely on fame or financial gain, Oprah consistently asks herself, "What's the intention behind this?" This mindful approach to goal setting has allowed her to create a career that not only brought her external success but also deep personal fulfillment.[41]

Scientific Insight: Research published in the journal "Psychology of Well-Being" found that individuals who set goals aligned with their intrinsic values experience greater levels of happiness and motivation. When your goals are rooted in mindfulness and authenticity, you're more likely to stay committed to them, even when faced with challenges.[42]

Practical Insight: The next time you set a goal, take a moment to ask yourself these questions:

- "Does this goal reflect my core values?"

- "How will pursuing this goal contribute to my overall well-being?"

- "Is this goal motivated by my own desires or by the expectations of others?"

By setting goals mindfully, you ensure that your pursuit of success feels authentic, purposeful, and aligned with who you are.

Presence in the Process

Success is not just about reaching the destination—it's about how you experience the journey. One of the most profound gifts of mindfulness is that it allows you to stay present throughout the process, enabling you to appreciate each step and learn from every experience. This presence helps you avoid burnout and ensures that your journey toward success is enriching, rather than exhausting.

Example: Renowned author and motivational speaker Brené Brown practices mindfulness to stay grounded and present in her work. Despite her busy schedule, Brown makes a conscious effort to engage fully in each task, whether she's writing, speaking, or spending time with her family. This mindfulness helps her stay connected to the joy of her work and avoid being consumed by the pressure of external demands.[43]

Scientific Insight: A study conducted by the "Harvard Business Review" found that employees who practice mindfulness report higher levels of job satisfaction and productivity. When you're fully present, you're more engaged, less prone to distractions, and able to produce higher-quality work.[44]

Practical Insight: Incorporate the practice of "micro-mindfulness" into your day. This means finding small moments to be fully present, such as taking a few deep breaths before starting a task, savoring your morning coffee without distractions, or engaging in a short meditation during a break. These brief moments of mindfulness can help you reconnect with the present moment, making your work feel more meaningful and less overwhelming.

Putting It All Together: Mindfulness as a Pathway to Authentic Success

By integrating mindfulness into your daily decisions, goal-setting, and overall journey, you create a foundation of inner peace that supports sustainable success. Mindfulness isn't about slowing down your progress or diluting your ambition; it's about ensuring that every action you take is rooted in intention, clarity, and alignment with your true self. It transforms your pursuit of success from a frantic race into a purposeful journey, where each step feels meaningful and enriching.

As you continue to cultivate mindfulness, you'll discover that success is not just about what you achieve but about how you experience the process. You'll find greater fulfillment, creativity, and resilience as you navigate the inevitable challenges along the way. Most importantly, you'll realize that by staying present and mindful, you're not just achieving success—you're living it.

Action Step: Creating a Success and Peace Alignment Framework

In this chapter, we explored how inner peace and success can support each other. Now it's time to put this into action with a simple framework to align your goals with your inner sense of peace.

1. **Clarify Your Core Values**: Start by writing down your top three values—these are the principles that are most important to you in life. They might include things like family, creativity, integrity, health, or freedom. Identifying your core values will serve as a foundation for aligning your ambitions with what truly matters to you.

2. **Define Your Vision of Success**: Take a moment to think about what success means to you. How can you pursue your goals while maintaining your peace? Write a short statement describing your personal vision of success that integrates both your ambitions and your well-being.

3. **Align Your Goals with Your Values**: Look at your current goals. Do they reflect your core values? If not, consider how you can adjust them or approach them differently to ensure they're in line with what matters most to you. This might mean redefining your goals or setting new priorities that honor both your drive and your inner peace.

4. **Evaluate Your Daily Actions**: At the end of each day, take a few moments to reflect on how your actions aligned with your values and goals. Were there times when stress or external pressures pulled you away from your sense of peace? How can you handle those situations differently moving forward?

5. **Incorporate Mindfulness into Your Routine:** Choose one daily activity—whether it's your morning routine, a meeting, or a task at work—and approach it with mindfulness. Be fully present and notice how this shifts your experience, helping you maintain a sense of peace throughout your day.

Ethan in Action: Putting It All Together

Ethan's journey continued to unfold as he navigated the realities of balancing his ambitions with a newfound sense of inner calm. One morning, as he faced an overflowing to-do list, he felt that familiar rush of anxiety creeping in. There were urgent emails, tight deadlines, and a major presentation to prepare. In the past, he would have let the pressure take over, pushing himself to power through the stress. But now, he took a deep breath, grounding himself in the moment. Instead of diving headfirst into the chaos, he paused and asked himself what was truly important. Ethan started with the tasks that mattered most, rather than allowing himself to be overwhelmed by everything at once. This simple act helped him approach his work with a sense of clarity and purpose that had been missing before.

A few days later, Ethan found himself facing an important opportunity. He'd been working on a pitch for a potential client that could open new doors for his company. As the day of the presentation approached, he felt the urge to stay up all night, refining every last detail to ensure perfection. This time, instead of slipping back into his old habits, he decided to take a step back. He went for a walk, letting his mind rest and giving himself space to breathe. It was during that walk that he realized the pitch didn't need to be flawless; it needed to be authentic and true to his vision. When he returned to his work, he felt more grounded and confident, ready to share his ideas without the weight of unnecessary pressure. The pitch went well, and the client *appreciated not only his ideas but also the calm and assured way he presented them.*

Looking back on the past few weeks, Ethan began to see the shifts taking root in his life. He was still ambitious, still striving to excel, but his approach had changed. Success was no longer about reaching a specific destination; it was about how he handled the journey. He realized that the balance between peace and ambition wasn't an either-or choice but rather two forces that could work together. By embracing this new perspective, Ethan discovered that he could be driven and centered, that he could achieve his goals without burning out, and that, in many ways, his most meaningful successes came from approaching his work with a sense of balance and authenticity.

Ethan's story was far from over, but it was clear that he was becoming someone who understood that real success wasn't just about the milestones—it was about who he was becoming along the way.

Summary: The Interplay Between Success and Peace

In this chapter, we dismantled the myth that success and inner peace are incompatible, showing that they can, in fact, coexist and even amplify each other. The chapter illustrates how integrating inner peace into the pursuit of success doesn't mean compromising ambition but rather enhances decision-making, resilience, and creativity.

Key Takeaways

- Inner peace and success are not mutually exclusive; they can coexist and support one another.

- Mindfulness serves as a powerful tool for aligning ambitions with core values, leading to more meaningful achievements.

- By approaching success from a place of balance and clarity, one's journey becomes more sustainable and fulfilling.

Conclusion: Success That's Worth Pursuing

The journey toward success becomes infinitely more fulfilling when guided by inner peace. It's no longer about relentlessly chasing goals but about pursuing them with intention, clarity, and balance. As Ethan's story reveals, achieving success doesn't have to mean sacrificing your well-being. Instead, it's about finding harmony between ambition and inner tranquility.

When you prioritize your values and align them with your aspirations, your path becomes clearer and more meaningful. Inner peace provides the foundation that allows you to navigate challenges with resilience and grace, leading to a deeper sense of fulfillment and purpose.

As we move forward, we'll explore how to cultivate resilience without losing this sense of balance—a vital skill for staying grounded as you continue to chase your dreams. In the next chapter, you'll discover how embracing resilience, not just as a form of toughness but as a practice of inner strength, can further enrich your journey toward sustainable success.

Five

✿

Building Resilience Without Losing Peace

Ethan stood at a crossroads, staring at a screen filled with reminders of tasks that needed completion. A year ago, he would have tackled them head-on, fueled by an urgent need to prove himself. But now, something had shifted. He took a deep breath and reminded himself of the lessons he'd learned—the importance of inner peace, balance, and self-awareness.

The pressures of his job hadn't lessened. In fact, they had intensified with new responsibilities and bigger expectations. Yet, Ethan was no longer the person who would sacrifice his well-being for the sake of meeting every demand. He had begun to understand that true resilience wasn't about pushing through at all costs but about learning how to bend without breaking.

One morning, as he was preparing for an important presentation, Ethan felt the familiar twinge of anxiety. The stakes were high, and the pressure to perform was immense. In the past, he would have allowed this feeling to take over, driving him to work late into the night and skip meals. But this time, he decided to approach the situation differently. He took a moment to breathe, closing his eyes and focusing on the steady rhythm of his breath, allowing himself to find a sense of calm amidst the chaos.

As the day progressed, Ethan faced setbacks: last-minute changes, unexpected challenges, and moments where he doubted his abilities. But instead of succumbing to the stress, he chose to respond with patience and self-compassion. He paused to reflect, reminding himself that resilience wasn't about avoiding failure but about how he chose to rise after each stumble.

After the presentation, which went better than expected, Ethan felt a deep sense of gratitude—not just for the success but for how he had approached the challenge—with a sense of balance and peace. He was beginning to see that his greatest strength wasn't in his ability to hustle but in his capacity to stay grounded, even when faced with adversity.

Introduction: Resilience as a Path to Inner Strength

Life is unpredictable, and no matter how much we prepare or plan, challenges will inevitably arise. Setbacks, failures, and unexpected difficulties are part of every journey toward success. Yet, it's how we respond to these challenges that determines whether we emerge stronger or feel defeated.

Resilience—the ability to recover quickly from setbacks—is an essential trait for anyone pursuing success. However, many people associate resilience with "toughing it out" or pushing through challenges at the cost of their well-being. In this chapter, we'll explore a different approach: how to build resilience without losing your inner peace. True resilience doesn't come from denying your emotions or fighting against adversity; it comes from learning to navigate challenges with grace, clarity, and emotional strength.

Rather than seeing resilience as a battle against life's obstacles, what if we viewed it as a dance? Like a tree that bends in the wind without breaking, resilient individuals learn to adapt, grow, and find strength in the very challenges that might once have threatened to uproot them. This adaptability allows us to face difficulties not with rigid resistance but with a spirit of curiosity and acceptance. It's in these moments of adversity that we often discover our greatest sources of strength, the depth of our inner peace, and the power of self-compassion.

By cultivating resilience, you're not just surviving the storms—you're learning to thrive within them. This chapter will guide you through the process of building resilience in a way that respects your emotional well-being and helps you maintain your sense of inner peace. You'll discover that resilience isn't about ignoring your pain or pushing through exhaustion; it's about acknowledging your vulnerabilities, accepting the present moment, and finding the courage to rise again with greater wisdom and strength.

Resilience, when rooted in inner peace, becomes more than just a coping mechanism; it transforms into a path toward deeper self-awareness and growth. It allows you to stay grounded when life's uncertainties threaten to knock you off course, reminding you that true strength lies not in avoiding challenges but in embracing them as opportunities to learn, grow, and become more fully yourself.

Redefining Resilience: Beyond Grit

In our culture, resilience is often framed as toughness or grit—the ability to endure hardship without breaking. While these qualities are admirable, they can also lead to burnout if misunderstood. Many people believe that resilience requires them to suppress their emotions, avoid vulnerability, or push forward no matter what. But true resilience is not about gritting your teeth through challenges—it's about adapting, recovering, and growing from them.

Resilience involves both strength and flexibility. Imagine a tree in a storm. The tree doesn't fight the wind; it bends, sways, and moves with the force of the storm. Yet, it remains firmly rooted, drawing strength from the ground below. This is how inner peace can help you become more resilient—by grounding yourself in peace, you can adapt to life's storms without losing your center.

True resilience is not found in resisting change but in learning to flow with it. When we view resilience solely as toughness, we risk becoming rigid and unyielding, which makes us more likely to break when life's pressures intensify. Instead, resilience is about embracing our vulnerabilities, acknowledging our fears, and allowing ourselves to experience emotions fully—even the uncomfortable ones. It's through this honest engagement with life's challenges that we build the capacity to respond with strength and grace.

Think about a time when you faced a setback—perhaps a failed project, a relationship that ended, or a goal that you failed to reach. In those moments, the instinct to power through or ignore your emotions might have felt like the right choice. However, it's often when we pause, reflect, and give ourselves permission to feel that we uncover the true source of our resilience. By allowing ourselves to bend rather than break, we gain a deeper understanding of our inner strength and the lessons each challenge offers.

Resilience also requires self-compassion. It's about recognizing that setbacks are not a sign of weakness but a natural part of the journey. When you approach challenges with self-compassion, you create space for growth and healing, which allows you to bounce back stronger. Instead of berating yourself for not meeting expectations or for feeling overwhelmed, resilience asks you to treat yourself with kindness, acknowledging that everyone faces difficulties and that every setback is an opportunity to learn and evolve.

This concept of resilience aligns perfectly with the idea of inner peace. When you cultivate inner peace, you create a steady foundation that supports you through life's storms. Inner peace doesn't eliminate challenges; it gives you the emotional stability to face them with clarity and courage. It allows you to respond thoughtfully instead of reacting impulsively, to adapt instead of resist, and to recover instead of retreat.

By redefining resilience, we shift from the exhausting pursuit of unyielding toughness to a more sustainable, compassionate approach to life's challenges. It's about understanding that resilience is not a fixed trait, but a skill that can be nurtured through self-awareness, adaptability, and a commitment to maintaining your inner peace. When you approach resilience in this way, you're no longer simply enduring life's storms— you're learning to dance in the rain, grounded in the knowledge that you have the strength to weather whatever comes your way.

The Role of Emotional Awareness in Resilience

One of the most critical aspects of resilience is emotional awareness. When faced with challenges, many of us default to one of two responses: suppression or overwhelm. We either try to ignore our feelings, pushing them aside to keep moving forward, or we become consumed by them, unable to function effectively. In both cases, we miss an opportunity to tap into the power that our emotions can offer us.

Inner peace teaches us a different way: to acknowledge and process our emotions without being controlled by them. Emotional awareness is the foundation of resilient behavior. By paying attention to how we feel—without judgment—we create the space to respond to difficulties with clarity and purpose rather than reacting out of stress or fear. This ability to be present with our emotions, even in the face of adversity, allows us to navigate life's challenges with a sense of grace and inner strength.

Embrace Your Emotions

Resilience begins with accepting your emotions, even the difficult ones. Feeling frustrated, sad, or disappointed doesn't make you weak—it makes you human. Each emotion you experience carries valuable information about your needs, desires, and values. By allowing yourself to feel these emotions, you become more attuned to what matters most to you and how you want to move forward. The key is to give yourself permission to experience these emotions without letting them dictate your actions or self-worth.

Consider the moments when you've faced a setback or encountered an unexpected obstacle. Instead of trying to "power through" and deny what you're feeling, try sitting with those emotions. Ask yourself: *What is this feeling trying to tell me? What can I learn from it?* This process of inquiry helps you develop a deeper understanding of yourself, making it easier to respond to challenges in a way that aligns with your values and goals.

Practical Exercise: Set aside a few minutes each day to check in with yourself. Find a quiet space, close your eyes, and ask, *"What am I feeling right now?"* Instead of labeling your emotions as "good" or "bad," simply observe them. This practice of non-judgmental awareness helps you build a more compassionate relationship with your emotions, allowing you to approach challenges with a sense of calm and clarity.

Respond, Don't React

Once you've acknowledged your emotions, the next step is to respond mindfully rather than react impulsively. When we react, we often do so out of habit, fear, or stress, which can lead to actions we later regret. Responding, on the other hand, requires a moment of pause—a chance to breathe and assess the situation before making decisions. This pause creates space between the emotion and the action, giving you the opportunity to choose how you want to move forward.

Imagine you're faced with harsh criticism at work. Your initial reaction might be to defend yourself or become angry. However, by taking a moment to pause, you can choose a more constructive response, such as asking for clarification, considering the feedback objectively, or acknowledging how the criticism makes you feel without letting it define you. This practice helps you maintain your inner peace and respond from a place of strength and intentionality.

Practical Insight: Whenever you feel triggered by a situation, take three deep breaths before responding. This simple technique helps regulate your nervous system, bringing you back to a state of calm and allowing you to approach the situation with greater clarity. Over time, this habit trains your mind to respond rather than react, making you more resilient in the face of challenges.

The Power of Self-Compassion

A crucial part of emotional awareness is the practice of self-compassion. Often, when faced with setbacks, we're our harshest critics, replaying our mistakes and shortcomings in our minds. But resilience isn't about being perfect—it's about treating ourselves with the same kindness and understanding we would offer a friend. By approaching ourselves with compassion, we create a safe space to explore our emotions and learn from them, rather than being overwhelmed by them.

When you're compassionate with yourself, you acknowledge that it's okay to feel hurt, disappointed, or anxious. These emotions are part of the human experience. Instead of trying to suppress them or beat yourself up for feeling them, you allow yourself to experience them fully, which is a vital step toward healing and growth.

Practical Insight: The next time you're feeling overwhelmed or critical of yourself, pause and ask, *"What would I say to a friend in this situation?"* Chances are, you'd offer words of encouragement, empathy, and support. Practice directing that same kindness toward yourself. This shift in perspective fosters a deeper sense of inner peace and strengthens your resilience over time.

Emotional Awareness as a Lifelong Practice

Emotional awareness isn't a skill you develop overnight; it's a lifelong practice. The more you engage with your emotions—listening to them, learning from them, and responding to them—the more resilient you become. You'll find that by staying present with your feelings, even when they're uncomfortable, you build the capacity to face challenges with courage and authenticity.

In time, this emotional awareness transforms your relationship with adversity. Instead of viewing challenges as threats to your stability, you begin to see them as opportunities for growth, self-discovery, and a deeper connection to your inner peace. When you cultivate emotional awareness, you strengthen the roots that anchor you, allowing you to bend but not break in the face of life's storms.

By integrating emotional awareness into your journey, you discover that resilience isn't about avoiding pain or discomfort but about embracing it as a necessary part of your growth. This awareness becomes your guiding light, helping you navigate even the most difficult moments with a sense of grace, clarity, and unwavering inner strength.

How Resilience and Peace Work Together

Inner peace and resilience are not separate concepts—they reinforce one another in powerful ways. Inner peace provides the calm and clarity needed to face challenges, while resilience ensures that you maintain that peace even in the midst of adversity. Together, they create a strong foundation that enables you to navigate life's difficulties with poise, strength, and a sense of purpose.

Here's how resilience and peace can work together:

Resilience as Adaptability

Inner peace helps you stay flexible in the face of obstacles. When you're at peace, you're less likely to be consumed by anxiety or fear, which allows you to adapt to changes without becoming overly attached to a specific outcome. This adaptability is a core component of resilience, enabling you to pivot and find new paths forward when your original plan encounters roadblocks.

For instance, consider working towards a long-term career goal and then facing an unexpected change, such as a job loss, a shift in market demand, or a failed project. Without inner peace, you might react with panic, frustration, or a sense of hopelessness, making it difficult to see any alternative paths. However, when grounded in inner peace, you're more likely to pause, breathe, and consider new possibilities. This mindset allows you to adapt to the change, explore different opportunities, or redefine your goals in a way that aligns with your true aspirations.

Practical Insight: The next time you face an obstacle, take a moment to identify any attachments you have to a particular outcome. Ask yourself, *"What can I learn from this situation? How can I adapt and move forward?"* By regularly practicing this shift in perspective, you strengthen your ability to stay flexible and resilient in the face of life's uncertainties.

Resilience as Acceptance

Inner peace fosters acceptance, which is a crucial part of resilience. Often, when faced with challenges, we waste valuable energy resisting reality or fighting against circumstances we cannot control. This resistance creates additional stress, making it harder to bounce back from setbacks. Inner peace, on the other hand, teaches us to accept what is without judgment or resistance.

Acceptance doesn't mean complacency or giving up; it means acknowledging the situation as it is and choosing your response consciously. It's about recognizing that while you may not have control over external events, you always have control over how you respond to them. This mindset shift allows you to face challenges with greater resilience, as you're no longer expending energy on things beyond your control.

For instance, if you experience a personal setback, such as a health issue or financial difficulty, acceptance allows you to confront the situation honestly and focus on what you can do to move forward. Instead of dwelling on why it happened or wishing things were different, you direct your energy toward finding solutions, seeking support, and taking positive steps to improve your circumstances.

Practical Insight: The next time you encounter a challenging situation, try the "Serenity Practice." Close your eyes, take a deep breath, and silently repeat the Serenity Prayer: *"Grant me the serenity to accept the things I cannot change, the courage to change the things I can, and the wisdom to know the difference."* This simple practice helps you cultivate acceptance, allowing you to face challenges with a sense of peace and resilience.

Resilience as Growth

Challenges are often our greatest teachers, offering opportunities for growth, self-discovery, and transformation. When you approach adversity with a mindset rooted in peace, you're more likely to extract valuable lessons from every setback. Instead of seeing failure as a defeat, you view it as an opportunity to learn, evolve, and become stronger. This mindset shift is critical to building resilience.

Consider an athlete who suffers an injury that temporarily halts their training. While the initial reaction might be frustration or disappointment, those who approach the situation with inner peace are more likely to see it as a chance to rest, reflect, and work on other aspects of their performance, such as mental conditioning or strategy. When they eventually return to their sport, they do so with renewed strength, insight, and resilience.

Similarly, in your own life, viewing setbacks as opportunities for growth allows you to approach challenges with curiosity rather than fear. It shifts your focus from *"Why did this happen to me?"* to *"What can I learn from this experience?"*

Practical Insight: Start a journal dedicated to tracking the challenges you face and the lessons you learn from them. After each setback, write down what happened, how you felt, and what insights you gained from the experience. Over time, you'll start to see how each challenge has contributed to your growth and resilience, reinforcing the idea that adversity can be a powerful catalyst for positive change.

The Dance Between Peace and Resilience

When inner peace and resilience work together, they create a dynamic, ever-evolving process that allows you to navigate life's challenges with confidence and grace. Inner peace provides the grounding you need to face difficulties without being overwhelmed, while resilience gives you the strength to maintain that peace, even when life feels chaotic.

This harmony transforms the way you approach adversity. Instead of viewing challenges as threats, you begin to see them as invitations to grow, adapt, and deepen your connection to yourself. You develop the capacity to face uncertainty with an open heart, trusting that no matter what happens, you have the strength, flexibility, and inner calm to weather any storm.

By cultivating both inner peace and resilience, you're not just surviving life's challenges—you're thriving in the midst of them. You become like that tree in the storm—firmly rooted, yet flexible enough to bend with the wind, knowing that every gust makes you stronger and more grounded in your journey.

Building Resilience Through Self-Compassion

One of the most overlooked aspects of resilience is self-compassion. When we face difficulties, our internal critic often becomes louder, telling us we've failed, we're not strong enough, or we should be doing better. This self-judgment only makes challenges harder to navigate, draining our energy and making it more difficult to recover. By embracing self-compassion, we cultivate a nurturing environment where resilience can flourish, allowing us to face setbacks with finese and understanding.

Self-compassion is the practice of treating yourself with the same kindness and understanding that you would offer a close friend. It's about recognizing that setbacks and struggles are part of the human experience and that you deserve care and patience as you navigate them. When you approach yourself with empathy, you create a space for healing, growth, and the development of true resilience.

Here's how self-compassion can enhance your resilience:

Silencing the Inner Critic

When you face setbacks, it's easy to spiral into negative self-talk. Thoughts like *"I should have done better,"* *"I'm not cut out for this,"* or *"I always mess up"* can quickly take over, feeding feelings of shame, inadequacy, and defeat. However, by practicing self-compassion, you can interrupt this cycle and offer yourself words of encouragement instead.

123

Start by acknowledging the critical voice in your head, but rather than accepting it as truth, challenge it. Ask yourself: *"Would I speak to a friend this way if they were in the same situation?"* The answer is almost always no. Replace those harsh words with kind, supportive statements like, *"It's okay to make mistakes; I'm learning,"* or *"I did my best given the circumstances."* This shift helps you maintain your confidence and sense of self-worth, even in the face of setbacks.

Practical Insight: When you catch yourself in the midst of negative self-talk, pause and take a self-compassion break. Place your hand on your heart, take a deep breath, and say to yourself:

- "This is a moment of suffering."

- "Suffering is a part of life."

- "May I be kind to myself in this moment."

This practice, developed by Dr. Kristin Neff, helps ground you in the present and reminds you that you deserve the same kindness you would offer to others.[45]

Allowing Space for Healing

Resilience doesn't mean bouncing back immediately—it means giving yourself the time and space to heal and recover. Often, we feel pressured to "get over" setbacks as quickly as possible, viewing any delay in recovery as a sign of weakness. But true resilience isn't about speed; it's about allowing yourself to move through the healing process at your own pace.

Self-compassion allows you to take that space without guilt, recognizing that rest is a necessary part of long-term success. Just as a wound needs time to heal, so do our emotional and mental scars. By honoring your need for rest, reflection, or even a temporary retreat, you build the strength to return to life's challenges with renewed energy and perspective.

Practical Insight: Identify a simple self-care ritual that you can turn to when you're feeling overwhelmed or in need of healing. It might be a warm bath, a walk in nature, listening to your favorite music, or practicing a hobby you love. This ritual serves as a reminder that it's okay to prioritize your well-being and that giving yourself space to heal is a vital part of resilience.

Reframing Failure

Rather than seeing failure as a reflection of your worth, self-compassion helps you reframe it as a natural part of the process. Every setback is a stepping stone toward greater understanding, and every failure offers lessons that can make you stronger. When you approach failure with self-compassion, you're more likely to view it as an opportunity for growth rather than a personal shortcoming.

For instance, consider an entrepreneur who launches a new business only to see it struggle or even fail within the first year. The immediate reaction might be one of disappointment, frustration, or self-doubt. However, by practicing self-compassion, they can step back and ask: *"What can I learn from this experience? How can I use this knowledge to improve in the future?"* This shift in mindset allows them to see failure not as an endpoint but as a valuable lesson on the path to success.

Practical Insight: After experiencing a setback, take a moment to write down what happened, how it made you feel, and most importantly, what you learned from the experience. This practice transforms failure into a learning opportunity and reinforces the idea that every challenge offers a chance to grow. Over time, you'll build a record of how setbacks have contributed to your personal development, making it easier to approach future challenges with resilience and self-compassion.

The Power of Self-Compassion in Daily Life

Incorporating self-compassion into your daily life builds an unshakeable foundation for resilience. It allows you to face challenges with a sense of understanding rather than judgment, to view setbacks as opportunities for growth rather than proof of inadequacy, and to offer yourself the kindness you need to navigate life's storms. As you practice self-compassion, you'll find that resilience doesn't require you to be invincible; it asks you to be human—to embrace your imperfections, honor your journey, and trust in your ability to rise, time and time again.

When you combine self-compassion with resilience, you transform your approach to adversity. You become someone who doesn't just endure challenges but learns, heals, and grows from them. And in doing so, you cultivate an inner strength that is rooted not in toughness or grit, but in the profound understanding that you are worthy of kindness, care, and the space to be yourself—no matter what life throws your way.

Action Step: Journaling for Resilience

A powerful way to cultivate both resilience and inner peace is through reflective journaling. This practice helps you process your emotions, gain clarity, and shift your perspective on challenges, allowing you to approach setbacks with greater compassion and adaptability. Here's an expanded journaling exercise to help you build resilience and integrate the lessons from this chapter:

1. Reflect on a Recent Challenge: Think about a challenge or setback you've faced recently. Write down the details of the situation, including how you felt, how you responded, and what thoughts or beliefs were triggered by the experience. Be as honest and detailed as possible, allowing yourself to acknowledge any emotions that surfaced.

2. Explore Your Emotional Awareness: Take some time to dig deeper into the emotions you experienced during this challenge. Were there moments when you tried to suppress or ignore your feelings? Did you allow yourself to experience them fully, or did you react impulsively? This step encourages emotional awareness, which is crucial for building resilience.

3. Reframe the Challenge for Growth: Now, reframe the challenge from a different perspective. Identify at least one lesson you learned or a way in which the experience contributed to your personal growth. Consider how the setback could serve as a stepping stone toward resilience, helping you become stronger and more adaptable.

4. Offer Yourself Compassionate Encouragement: Think about how you would support a friend who went through a similar experience. What words of encouragement, understanding, or kindness would you offer them? Now, direct those same words toward yourself, reinforcing the importance of self-compassion as you navigate life's challenges.

5. Identify an Actionable Step Forward: Reflect on how you can use this experience to move forward in a way that supports both your resilience and inner peace. Identify one small, actionable step you can take to handle similar challenges differently in the future.

Ethan in Action: Rising Stronger Through Setbacks

A month later, Ethan faced one of his biggest setbacks yet. A high-stakes marketing campaign he had poured countless hours into fell flat, failing to generate the expected results. Immediately, the familiar urge to fix everything himself kicked in. He contemplated staying up all night, overworking himself to salvage the project and regain his sense of control. The weight of disappointment pressed heavily on his shoulders, and self-doubt crept in.

But as he stared at his computer screen, Ethan paused. He recalled his commitment to building resilience in a way that honored his inner peace. Instead of giving in to the impulse to work harder, Ethan decided to take a step back and assess the situation from a place of calm. He reminded himself that resilience wasn't about gritting his teeth through adversity but about approaching challenges with a sense of adaptability and compassion.

Ethan stepped outside for a walk, allowing himself to process the sting of failure without judgment. As he strolled through a nearby park, he acknowledged the emotions swirling within him—frustration, disappointment, and even fear of what others might think. Instead of suppressing these feelings, he embraced them, reminding himself that setbacks were a natural part of growth. By allowing himself to experience his emotions, he was practicing self-compassion, which he had learned was crucial for developing true resilience.

When he returned to his office, Ethan took out his journal and began writing about the lessons he could learn from this experience. He reflected on what went wrong, what factors were within his control, and which were beyond it. As he wrote, he began to see the setback not as a reflection of his abilities but as an opportunity to adapt, grow, and refine his approach.

The next morning, Ethan returned to the project with a clearer mind. Rather than tackling the problem alone, he reached out to his team and invited them to discuss the campaign's shortcomings. He shared his reflections openly, admitting where he felt the campaign could have been stronger and encouraging his team to do the same. This vulnerability not only built trust, but also inspired a sense of camaraderie among his colleagues.

As they brainstormed together, new ideas emerged—ideas that Ethan might never have considered if he had simply tried to fix everything on his own. The project took on new life, and although they couldn't completely undo the setback, they were able to pivot and create a revised plan that was even more aligned with the team's strengths and insights.

In that moment, Ethan realized that resilience wasn't about avoiding failure but about responding to it with flexibility, self-compassion, and a willingness to grow. By choosing to respond with resilience and compassion rather than overworking himself, he discovered that setbacks didn't have to define him; they could be transformed into valuable opportunities for growth and connection.

This experience reinforced that resilience wasn't just about bouncing back—it was about bouncing forward, armed with the lessons learned and a deeper sense of inner peace.

Summary: Building Resilience Without Losing Peace

In this chapter, resilience is redefined as a journey of adaptability, emotional awareness, and self-compassion rather than mere grit and toughness. Readers learn that true resilience involves responding to challenges with flexibility, patience, and a commitment to inner peace, rather than pushing through at all costs. This chapter highlights that setbacks are not indicators of failure but opportunities for growth and learning. By cultivating self-compassion and emotional awareness, we can transform obstacles into valuable lessons and emerge stronger from them.

Key Takeaways

- Resilience is about adapting and growing from setbacks, not just pushing through them.

- Emotional awareness and self-compassion are crucial components of true resilience.

- Inner peace helps you stay grounded and focused in the face of challenges.

Conclusion: Embracing Resilience as a Path to Inner Strength

Resilience is not about powering through life's challenges with unyielding toughness; it's about learning to bend without breaking, adapting with grace, and growing stronger with every setback. By embracing emotional awareness, self-compassion, and the harmony between resilience and inner peace, you cultivate the ability to face adversity without losing yourself in the process.

As Ethan discovered, resilience is a skill that can be nurtured through mindful practices, patience, and a willingness to learn from life's inevitable challenges. It's not about avoiding failure or pain but about responding to them with clarity, courage, and compassion. When you approach life with this mindset, you transform obstacles into opportunities, setbacks into stepping stones, and challenges into moments of profound growth.

The path to resilience is a journey, one that invites you to be kind to yourself, stay present with your emotions, and trust in your ability to rise again. By integrating these lessons into your life, you'll find that resilience doesn't just help you survive life's storms—it empowers you to dance in the rain, grounded in your inner strength and peace.

Six

🪷

The Quiet Strength of Patience

Ethan sat at his desk, his fingers tapping rhythmically against the surface, eyes glued to the clock on his computer. *The email he had been waiting for all week hadn't come. A major project proposal was under review, and the client had promised feedback by the end of the day. But now it was nearly 6 p.m., and his inbox was still empty.*

His mind buzzed with frustration. Why are they taking so long? He had worked tirelessly on this project, pouring every ounce of energy into perfecting the proposal. His phone lit up with another message—a reminder of a meeting he hadn't had time to prepare for. His heart raced as he scrolled through his endless to-do list, feeling the weight of every task piling up.

For Ethan, waiting had never come easily. His world thrived on action—solving problems, meeting deadlines, and always staying one step ahead. Patience felt like a waste of time, especially in a career that demanded quick results. But as he sat there, watching the minutes pass, the tension built. Every unanswered email, every ticking second, chipped away at his focus.

By the time he finally stood to leave, his chest felt tight with anxiety. The proposal still hung in limbo, and Ethan couldn't shake the gnawing sense of failure, even though nothing had gone wrong. He had done his part, but the waiting—the not knowing—was unraveling him. He knew deep down that patience was something he struggled with, but he had never really thought about how much it impacted his peace, his decisions, or his well-being.

As he headed out the door, he realized this wasn't just about the proposal. It was about his constant drive to push forward, to stay in control, and to avoid stillness. Maybe it was time to figure out why waiting felt so unbearable—and what it would take to truly practice patience in his fast-moving world.

Introduction: Cultivating Patience in a Fast-Paced World

In the age of constant hustle, where we're encouraged to work faster, aim higher, and never stop, patience can feel like a luxury we can't afford. Society celebrates quick achievements, immediate results, and the relentless pursuit of success, leaving little room for pauses. The pressure to constantly achieve creates a mindset where waiting, pausing, or reflecting is often seen as weakness, a lack of ambition, or even failure. Yet, patience is one of the most critical skills we can develop—not only for managing stress, but also for achieving sustainable, long-term success.

Patience offers something hustle culture cannot: the ability to move through life with intention and clarity. It allows us to step back, assess the bigger picture, and make thoughtful decisions rather than being swept away by urgency or anxiety. In moments where we feel the pressure to act, patience reminds us that not all progress is immediate and that growth—both personal and professional—often requires time, persistence, and trust in the process.

Cultivating patience gives us the space to grow, reflect, and adjust course when necessary. It helps us respond to challenges with resilience instead of reacting impulsively. By slowing down, we gain a clearer sense of our values and what truly matters, rather than chasing after every milestone. Patience invites us to balance ambition with a deeper sense of fulfillment, to appreciate the journey as much as the destination.

In this space—between rushing to the finish line and embracing the process—we find peace, purpose, and sustainable success.

Understanding the Nature of Patience

Patience is often misunderstood. Many view it as passive, as if patience means doing nothing while waiting for things to happen. But in reality, patience is an active skill, one rooted in emotional regulation, self-awareness, and trust. It's the ability to stay calm and composed in the face of delays, setbacks, or frustrations, while keeping sight of the bigger picture. Patience is about creating space between the present moment and the impulse to react, allowing for more thoughtful, intentional responses.

At its core, patience is a form of resilience. It's the strength to delay immediate gratification, to endure discomfort, and to trust in the process even when results aren't visible right away. This trust doesn't mean ignoring challenges or avoiding action; it means understanding that growth and progress unfold in their own time. Patience empowers us to face obstacles without being overwhelmed by them, and to respond with grace rather than frustration when things don't go as planned.

In today's culture, where success is frequently measured by how quickly we achieve our goals or reach the next milestone, patience stands in stark contrast. The pressure to move fast often leads to reactive decision-making, burnout, and a sense of dissatisfaction, even when we reach our goals. But patience reminds us that real, meaningful progress takes time. It encourages us to focus on the quality of our actions, not just the speed of our results.

When we practice patience, we aren't just waiting idly—we are creating the conditions for deeper growth, clarity, and sustainable achievement. Patience allows us to pace ourselves, preserving energy and focus for what truly matters. Without it, we risk rushing through important decisions, burning out before we reach our goals, or losing sight of the larger vision. Ultimately, patience is a key to long-term success, because it teaches us to value the process, not just the outcome.

The Role of Patience in Decision-Making

Patience plays an essential role in decision-making, yet it's often overlooked in a culture that values speed and immediate action. When we feel pressured to make decisions quickly—whether it's to meet a deadline, respond to a problem, or simply keep pace with others—we tend to make reactive choices. These decisions are often driven by fear of failure, the need for control, or the anxiety of losing out on an opportunity. In such moments, we act not out of wisdom, but out of urgency, and that can lead to poor outcomes or regret.

Patience, however, shifts this dynamic. It allows us to create space between the pressure to act and the decision itself. Instead of reacting impulsively, patience gives us the time to pause, reflect, and approach decisions with clarity and intention. It encourages us to slow down and assess the situation from multiple angles, helping us avoid short-term fixes that may not serve our long-term well-being.

By giving yourself time to weigh your options, you cultivate mental and emotional space necessary for more thoughtful, intentional actions. This process of deliberate reflection helps you step away from the noise of fear or urgency, and instead make decisions aligned with your values and long-term goals. Patience doesn't mean avoiding difficult decisions or delaying action indefinitely. Instead, it allows you to act from a place of calm and clarity rather than from stress or anxiety.

For example, consider a major career decision—whether to take on a new role, make a significant investment, or pivot in a different direction. When approached with patience, this decision becomes less about what needs to happen right now and more about what will serve your future self. You can evaluate the risks and rewards with greater clarity, ensuring your choice supports your overall vision rather than fulfilling a fleeting need for control or validation.

Patience transforms your approach to decision-making. It frees you from the false urgency that often leads to rushed decisions and opens the door to greater wisdom, alignment, and satisfaction. By allowing yourself the time to take a step back, you make space for decisions that not only solve immediate problems but also support your long-term well-being and personal growth.

Patience as an Antidote to Anxiety

Much of the anxiety we experience stems from a need to control outcomes, coupled with the pressure to achieve success as quickly as possible. When we're constantly rushing toward the next milestone, driven by the fear of missing opportunities or falling behind, we create a perpetual state of unease. The faster we push ourselves, the more our minds become consumed with worry—*what if we don't succeed? What if the timing isn't right? What if our best efforts aren't enough?*

Impatience thrives in this environment of uncertainty, feeding off the fear of the unknown. It pushes us to act, to force progress, as though any delay will cause everything to fall apart. This mindset not only amplifies stress but also disconnects us from the present moment. We find ourselves caught in a cycle of anticipation and anxiety, always focused on what's next, never fully experiencing or appreciating what's happening now. When we're in a constant state of "what if," we leave little room for reflection, gratitude, or rest—three essential components of peace.

Patience, however, offers an antidote to this cycle. It teaches us to release the need for immediate results and to trust that everything is unfolding as it should. Patience allows us to step back and embrace the uncertainty that once caused anxiety. By doing so, we begin to understand that progress doesn't always happen on our preferred timeline—and that's okay.

When we cultivate patience, we create space for calm and balance. The act of waiting, when coupled with trust, becomes less about passively enduring delays and more about actively choosing peace over pressure. We realize that immediate action doesn't always yield better outcomes, and that sometimes, the best course of action is to let things unfold naturally. This shift in mindset helps alleviate the constant pressure to perform, as we begin to focus less on forcing success and more on allowing things to take shape in their own time.

Patience also reduces the need to control every outcome, freeing us from the exhausting cycle of worry. It invites us to lean into uncertainty without fear, knowing that not every question needs an answer right away, and not every goal needs to be reached immediately. This newfound trust doesn't mean abandoning ambition—it means finding peace in the process rather than only in the results.

By embracing patience, we open ourselves to the present moment, reducing anxiety and cultivating a deeper sense of peace. It gives us permission to breathe, reflect, and trust that what we are working toward will come to fruition when the time is right. In this way, patience becomes a powerful tool for managing anxiety, fostering resilience, and creating a more balanced, intentional approach to life.

Building Patience Through Mindfulness

Mindfulness is one of the most effective tools for cultivating patience. In a world that constantly urges us to focus on what's next, mindfulness trains the mind to stay rooted in the present. It helps us resist the urge to rush ahead, allowing us to be fully aware of where we are, rather than always thinking about where we're going. Through mindfulness, we develop the ability to slow down, breathe, and observe our thoughts and emotions without reacting impulsively or letting stress dictate our responses. In this way, mindfulness builds the foundation for patience by helping us create space between a situation and our reaction to it.

When we practice mindfulness, we strengthen our capacity to be patient with ourselves, with others, and with life's unfolding. It invites us to embrace the moment we are in rather than perpetually striving for the next milestone. This practice shifts our focus from controlling the pace of everything around us to simply observing it with acceptance. The more we practice staying present, the more patience becomes a natural part of how we respond to challenges, delays, and stress.

Here are two key mindfulness practices that directly cultivate patience:

Breathing Exercises

One of the simplest and most powerful ways to cultivate patience is through mindful breathing. When we're faced with frustration, stress, or delays, our nervous system tends to go into overdrive, triggering impatience or anxiety. By focusing on your breath, you can instantly calm this physiological response, giving your mind and body the time to settle before reacting.[46]

Practical Insight: When you notice impatience or frustration building—whether you're waiting in line, dealing with a work setback, or having a difficult conversation—try focusing on your breath to anchor yourself in the present moment. Take a slow, deep breath, hold it for a few seconds, then exhale slowly. Repeat this process until you feel your body start to relax. This simple breathing exercise acts as a reset button for your nervous system, helping you respond with calmness and patience instead of reacting impulsively.

Over time, mindful breathing can become your go-to strategy for managing impatience in stressful situations. By practicing it regularly, you'll find it easier to pause before reacting, which strengthens your ability to handle delays and frustrations with greater patience.

Body Awareness

Impatience often manifests physically in the body before we even recognize it mentally. Your shoulders may tense, your jaw may tighten, or your stomach may clench, all signaling stress and impatience. By practicing body awareness, you can catch these physical signs early and release them before they escalate into frustration or anxiety.

Practical Insight: Make it a habit to check in with your body throughout the day. Start from the top of your head and work your way down, noticing any areas of tension or discomfort. For example, if you feel tension in your neck or shoulders, take a moment to stretch, breathe deeply, and release the tightness. You can also practice progressive muscle relaxation, where you tense and relax each muscle group, helping you release built-up stress.

Becoming more aware of where your body holds tension allows you to intervene before impatience takes over. It's a simple, mindful way to restore calm and patience in moments when you're feeling overwhelmed or stressed.

Integrating Mindfulness into Daily Life

To cultivate patience through mindfulness, it's important to integrate these practices into your daily routine, not just during moments of high stress. Here are some additional ways to build patience through mindful living:

- **Mindful Transitions:** Use small, everyday moments—such as walking from your car to your office, washing dishes, or taking a shower—as opportunities to practice mindfulness. Focus on the task at hand, paying attention to each movement and sensation. These brief pauses throughout the day remind you to stay present, cultivating patience over time.

- **Daily Reflection:** At the end of each day, take a few minutes to reflect on how you responded to challenges. Were there moments when you reacted out of impatience? How could you have used mindfulness to create more space between your feelings and your reaction? This self-awareness will deepen your ability to practice patience in future situations.

- **Gratitude for the Present:** Impatience often comes from wanting to fast-forward to the next goal or achievement. Practice gratitude by pausing to appreciate where you are now. What have you accomplished today? What small moments brought you peace or joy? Gratitude for the present helps shift your focus away from what's next and toward a deeper appreciation for the journey you're on.

By incorporating these mindfulness practices into your daily life, you strengthen your ability to stay present, even in moments of frustration or challenge. This not only enhances your capacity for patience but also deepens your connection to yourself, to those around you, and to the moment at hand. Over time, mindfulness helps you cultivate a more patient, peaceful way of moving through the world, allowing you to meet life's demands with calm and clarity, rather than haste or stress.

Patience and Ambition: A Balanced Approach

One of the greatest challenges we face in today's fast-paced culture is finding the balance between patience and ambition. We're constantly bombarded with messages that equate success with speed—the faster you achieve, the more accomplished you are. Hustle culture glorifies the idea that progress should be immediate and relentless, pushing us to constantly reach for the next goal, often without pausing to reflect on whether the pursuit is aligned with our deeper values or long-term fulfillment.

But the truth is, this mindset often leads to burnout, dissatisfaction, and a sense of emptiness. Chasing external markers of success—whether it's promotions, accolades, or financial gain—without ever feeling a sense of peace or contentment leaves us in a perpetual state of striving. We become so focused on the next win that we lose sight of the journey itself, and the achievements we do reach often feel hollow because they were attained through unsustainable effort.

Patience, however, doesn't mean sacrificing ambition. It's not about slowing down your goals or diminishing your drive—it's about pacing yourself. True ambition isn't measured by how fast you can achieve; it's measured by how deeply your goals align with your values and how intentionally you pursue them. Patience is what allows you to pursue your ambitions with endurance and mindfulness, understanding that real, lasting success comes from sustained effort, not from quick wins.

When you cultivate patience alongside your ambition, you allow yourself the time and space to grow in meaningful ways. This approach transforms the pursuit of success from a frantic race into a thoughtful, intentional journey. It encourages you to be more mindful about the decisions you make and to trust that progress will come in its own time—sometimes slowly, but steadily.

Patience reminds us that the journey is just as important as the destination. By pacing yourself, you avoid the trap of burnout, where constant striving leads to exhaustion, frustration, and ultimately a sense of disconnection from your original purpose. Ambition fueled by patience becomes a sustainable force—it allows you to pursue your goals without depleting your energy, losing focus, or compromising your well-being.

In practice, this means recognizing that not everything needs to be done right now. You don't need to check every box at once or achieve every goal immediately. Instead, you can approach your ambitions with the understanding that long-term success is built over time, with persistence and thoughtful effort. Patience creates room for flexibility, adaptation, and learning from setbacks—qualities that are essential for achieving true fulfillment.

Consider how this balanced approach might look in your own life. What would happen if you gave yourself permission to pursue your goals with both urgency and patience? If you allowed yourself to rest, reflect, and adjust course along the way? By adopting this mindset, you give yourself the freedom to enjoy the process of growth, rather than constantly chasing outcomes. In doing so, you not only achieve more meaningful success, but you also find peace and satisfaction in the journey itself.

Integrating Patience into Your Ambition

Balancing patience with ambition requires a shift in mindset—one that prioritizes long-term growth over short-term rewards. By integrating patience into your pursuit of success, you not only safeguard your well-being but also create space for more thoughtful, sustainable progress. Patience doesn't diminish your ambition; rather, it allows you to pursue your goals with greater clarity, purpose, and resilience. Here are three key ways to cultivate patience while staying focused on your ambitions:

- **Long-Term Perspective:** Shift your focus from short-term gains to long-term fulfillment. Ask yourself, *How do my current actions contribute to my larger vision?* Patience encourages you to look beyond immediate results and consider the lasting impact of your choices.

- **Sustainable Effort:** Recognize that sustainable success requires steady, consistent effort. Instead of sprinting toward every goal, pace yourself. Break larger goals into smaller, manageable steps and trust that progress will come with time and persistence.

- **Mindful Ambition:** Make time for reflection as you pursue your ambitions. Regularly check in with yourself to ensure that your actions are aligned with your values and that you're not sacrificing your well-being in the name of success. Mindful ambition is about moving forward with intention and clarity, not just speed.

Balancing patience with ambition is not about slowing down your drive—it's about sustaining it. By integrating patience into your pursuit of success, you create a more thoughtful, intentional, and ultimately fulfilling path forward. You're reminded that while achieving your goals is important, how you get there matters just as much.

Action Steps: Cultivating Patience in a Fast-Paced World

Patience is a skill that requires practice and intentionality. By incorporating these steps into your daily life, you can build a more patient, thoughtful approach to both your personal and professional goals. These practices are designed to help you slow down, reflect, and create space for more meaningful, sustainable progress.

1. **Mindful Breathing for Patience:** When you feel impatience rising—whether waiting for an email response, managing a work delay, or dealing with a personal frustration—pause and focus on your breath. Practice the 4-4-4 method: inhale deeply for 4 counts, hold for 4 counts, and exhale for 4 counts. Repeat this cycle 3-5 times, allowing your body to relax and your mind to settle. Use this moment to ground yourself, reset your nervous system, and approach the situation with greater calm and clarity.

2. **Daily Patience Reflection:** At the end of each day, take a few minutes to reflect on moments where you felt impatient. Write down what triggered the feeling and how you responded. Then, think

about how you could have integrated patience into the situation. What would a more measured response have looked like? Reflecting on these moments regularly helps you build self-awareness, recognize patterns, and gradually shift your reactions in future situations.

3. **Break Goals into Smaller Steps:** Rather than sprinting toward your long-term ambitions, break larger goals into smaller, manageable steps. Write down the smaller milestones and set realistic timelines for each one. This approach helps you pace yourself and prevents the overwhelm that often leads to impatience. Trust that meaningful progress takes time and celebrate each small step forward as part of the bigger journey.

4. **Set Boundaries to Prevent Burnout:** Impatience often arises from taking on too much too quickly. Set clear boundaries in your personal and professional life to protect your energy. Whether it's saying no to additional tasks or carving out time for rest, setting boundaries allows you to focus on your priorities without feeling rushed or overwhelmed. By pacing yourself, you cultivate a more sustainable path to success and peace.

5. **Gratitude for the Present Moment:** Impatience can stem from constantly focusing on the next achievement. To counter this, practice gratitude by appreciating where you are now. Each day, write down three things you are grateful for—whether it's a completed task, a meaningful conversation, or a small moment of

peace. This practice shifts your mindset from constantly striving to appreciating the present, which fosters a deeper sense of patience.

Ethan in Action: Finding Strength in Patience

Months had passed since that restless evening when Ethan had struggled with the weight of waiting. *His journey to practice patience was still ongoing, but today, something felt different.*

Ethan sat in a conference room, waiting to present his latest project. Unlike before, the pressure didn't feel overwhelming. The client was running late, and instead of anxiously checking his watch or scrolling through his phone, Ethan sat calmly, reviewing his notes with focus and clarity. He had learned that impatience wouldn't bring his client into the room any faster. The only thing within his control was how he chose to spend this moment. He closed his laptop and breathed deeply, centering himself.

This time, he wasn't just waiting; he was present, allowing himself to embrace the moment. He thought about how he had shifted his mindset over the past few months—letting go of the need to control every outcome and trusting that his work would speak for itself. He had started integrating mindfulness into his daily routine, taking time to pause and reflect, practicing deep breathing before meetings, and checking in with himself when stress arose.

Patience no longer felt like a passive skill. Instead, it had become a source of quiet strength. By pacing himself and focusing on sustainable progress, Ethan noticed that his approach to work—and life—had shifted. He wasn't as reactive as before, and even when deadlines loomed, he found himself making more thoughtful decisions rather than rushing to check off every task.

As the client finally arrived, Ethan greeted them with a calm confidence. The meeting unfolded smoothly, not because everything went perfectly, but because he was no longer tethered to perfection. He had given himself permission to slow down, to trust the process, and to focus on the value of the work itself, not just the speed of its delivery.

Later that evening, Ethan reflected on the day. The old version of himself would have been tense and frazzled, but now, he felt grounded. He was no longer racing against the clock, but moving forward with intention and clarity. Patience had become more than a tool for managing stress—it had become his guide in pursuing both ambition and peace.

As he packed up for the day, Ethan smiled. The project wasn't just a success because it went well; it was a success because he had grown. Patience had taught him that true achievement wasn't just about what he accomplished—it was about how he experienced the journey along the way.

Summary: The Power of Patience

In a culture that celebrates speed and instant results, patience can feel counterintuitive, yet it is one of the most powerful tools we can cultivate for long-term success and inner peace. Patience allows us to slow down, reflect, and approach challenges with clarity and resilience. It's a skill that helps us make better decisions, manage anxiety, and balance ambition with well-being.

Through the practice of patience, we learn to trust the process, embrace the present moment, and find value in the journey rather than simply the destination. This shift in mindset not only leads to more sustainable progress but also fosters a deeper sense of fulfillment.

Key Takeaways

- Patience isn't about doing nothing—it's about creating space to think, reflect, and respond thoughtfully. It helps us navigate setbacks and delays with grace while staying focused on our long-term goals.

- By allowing ourselves time to pause and reflect, patience leads to wiser, more intentional decisions. It gives us the clarity to act from a place of calm rather than urgency, aligning our choices with our values and long-term vision.

- The pressure to control outcomes and achieve quickly creates stress. Patience teaches us to let go of that need for control, embrace uncertainty, and trust that everything will unfold in its own time. This reduces anxiety and helps us focus on what we can manage.

- Incorporating mindfulness practices like deep breathing and body awareness helps cultivate patience by training the mind to stay present and calm in moments of frustration or stress. This practice enhances our ability to handle challenges without reacting impulsively.

- Patience doesn't diminish ambition—it enhances it. By pacing ourselves and focusing on long-term progress rather than short-term wins, we create a sustainable approach to success that aligns with our deeper values and goals.

Conclusion: Embracing the Quiet Strength of Patience

Patience may feel elusive in a world driven by constant hustle, but it is one of the most valuable tools we can cultivate for both success and peace. Throughout this chapter, we've explored how patience is not about passivity, but about creating space for reflection, thoughtful decision-making, and sustainable growth. It helps us navigate delays and setbacks with grace, manage the anxiety that stems from a need for control, and maintain a balanced approach to our ambitions.

By integrating patience into your life—through mindfulness, intentional action, and a shift in perspective—you'll find that the journey toward your goals becomes more fulfilling. The pursuit of success no longer feels rushed or reactive, but calm, focused, and aligned with your core values.

But while patience lays the foundation for a more intentional path, it's only part of the equation. As we move forward, we'll explore the critical balance between ambition and self-care. How can you keep striving for your goals without sacrificing your well-being? In the next chapter, discover how embracing rest and renewal can supercharge your ambition, creating a path to success that is both sustainable and deeply fulfilling.

Seven

✿

Balancing Ambition with Self-Care

Ethan had been making significant progress in redefining his approach to success, but a new challenge soon arose. With the company expanding, Ethan was given the chance to lead a major initiative—one that could position him as a frontrunner for a promotion he had long envisioned. The offer was tempting, but he knew that accepting it without boundaries could draw him back into the exhausting cycle he was trying to escape.

As Ethan reviewed the details of the new project, he felt the familiar tug of ambition urging him to dive in without hesitation. Yet, he paused and asked himself, "What have I learned about balancing ambition with self-care?" He realized that he could no longer afford to chase success at the expense of his well-being. This time, he wanted to prove that it was possible to pursue his goals without sacrificing his peace.

157

Determined to apply what he had learned, Ethan began by setting clear boundaries around his work hours. Instead of working late into the night as he would have in the past, he committed to ending his workday by a reasonable time, giving himself space to unwind. He also decided to start his mornings differently, taking 15 minutes each day for meditation or a mindful walk, allowing himself to center his thoughts before diving into the demands of the day.

Introduction: The Myth of "Either-Or"

Many of us have been taught to believe that we must choose between ambition and self-care and that we can't pursue big goals without sacrificing our health, happiness, or personal life. This is the core of hustle culture's message: success demands sacrifice, and the more you give up, the more you'll achieve. But what if the opposite were true? What if taking care of yourself wasn't a distraction from your goals, but a critical part of achieving them?

Imagine a version of success where you don't have to choose between your dreams and your well-being, where your journey to the top is not defined by exhaustion, burnout, or relentless stress. What if you could achieve more by giving yourself permission to rest, recharge, and nurture your mind, body, and spirit? When we shift our mindset from one of scarcity—believing we have to "do it all" at any cost—to one of abundance, we realize that self-care is not the enemy of ambition; it's the fuel that keeps it alive.

In this chapter, we'll explore how balancing ambition with self-care not only prevents burnout but also enhances your productivity, creativity, and overall well-being. By creating a sustainable lifestyle where success and self-care coexist, you'll discover that nurturing yourself doesn't detract from your goals; it propels you toward them with greater energy, clarity, and resilience. Together, we'll redefine what it means to be truly successful, embracing a path where your well-being is the foundation upon which your ambitions can thrive.

The Cost of Ignoring Self-Care

The modern workplace often glorifies overworking, equating longer hours with greater success. We're taught that pushing through exhaustion, sacrificing sleep, and ignoring our own needs is the price we must pay to reach the top. However, the cost of neglecting self-care is steep and often goes unnoticed until it's too late. Over time, ignoring your physical, mental, and emotional needs doesn't just lead to burnout; it drains your creativity, dulls your motivation, and strips away your sense of fulfillment. What was once a passionate pursuit becomes a relentless grind.

Burnout is not just physical exhaustion—it's an emotional and mental state of depletion. When you're burned out, everything feels like a grind, even the work that once brought you joy. Tasks that used to excite you feel burdensome, and the passion that fueled your ambition is replaced with a sense of dread or indifference. You may find yourself disconnected from your goals, questioning why you started in the first place. This erosion of enthusiasm doesn't just impact your work; it spills over into other areas of your life, affecting your relationships, health, and overall happiness.

Research has shown that chronic stress, a hallmark of ignoring self-care, can lead to a host of health issues, such as heart disease, weakened immune function, anxiety, and depression. It impairs your cognitive abilities, making it harder to concentrate, solve problems, or think creatively. Instead of being at your best, you're constantly operating in survival mode, running on fumes and unable to tap into your full potential.[47]

What's even more insidious is that burnout can create a cycle of diminishing returns. The more exhausted you become, the less effective and productive you are, which often leads to working even harder to compensate for the decreased output. This vicious cycle only accelerates the path to burnout, leaving you feeling stuck, unfulfilled, and wondering where it all went wrong.

This is why balancing ambition with self-care is essential. True success isn't measured by how much you can endure or how many hours you can log—it's about how effectively you can pursue your goals while maintaining your well-being. When you prioritize self-care, you're not taking time away from your ambitions; you're investing in your ability to sustain them. You're giving yourself the energy, clarity, and resilience needed to face challenges, stay inspired, and continue growing.

By nurturing yourself along the journey, you build a foundation that allows your ambition to thrive, not just in the short term but over the long haul. Remember, self-care is not a luxury or an afterthought; it's a crucial element of sustained success. Without it, even the greatest dreams can become burdens, and the journey tow7ard them can feel like an endless uphill climb.

Why Self-Care Fuels Ambition

Self-care isn't just about relaxation or indulgence; it's about preserving and restoring your energy so you can show up as your best self in all areas of life. Taking time for yourself isn't an obstacle to success—it's a way to ensure you have the clarity, focus, and stamina to pursue your goals with intention and resilience. When you make self-care a priority, you're not just recharging your batteries; you're investing in your ability to sustain your drive, creativity, and passion over the long term.

Here's why self-care fuels ambition:

Physical Well-Being and Energy

Your body is the vehicle that allows you to pursue your goals. When you prioritize sleep, nutrition, and exercise, you're ensuring that you have the energy to tackle challenges and stay focused. Think of your body as the engine that drives your ambition—if you don't fuel it properly, it will eventually break down.

For instance, research consistently shows that a lack of sleep impairs cognitive function, decision-making, and problem-solving skills. It's tempting to cut back on rest to squeeze in more work, but over time, this strategy backfires, leading to decreased productivity and increased stress. By prioritizing quality sleep, nourishing your body with healthy foods, and incorporating regular exercise, you enhance your ability to perform at your best, no matter how demanding your goals may be.[48]

Practical Insight: Start by making small adjustments to your routine, such as setting a consistent bedtime, taking short walks during breaks, or preparing nutritious meals in advance. These changes will have a cumulative effect, helping you maintain your energy and stamina as you pursue your ambitions.

Mental Clarity and Focus

Self-care practices like mindfulness, meditation, and rest help clear mental clutter, allowing you to focus on what's truly important. When your mind is clear, you can make better decisions, solve problems more effectively, and maintain perspective during stressful times. In a world full of distractions and constant demands, carving out time to quiet your mind can be the difference between feeling overwhelmed and staying grounded.

Many successful individuals, from entrepreneurs to athletes, swear by mindfulness techniques as a way to stay present and focused. By engaging in regular meditation, journaling, or even taking a few moments each day to breathe deeply, you create space in your mind to process information, gain insights, and approach challenges with a sense of calm.

Practical Insight: Incorporate a daily mindfulness practice, even if it's just for five minutes. Over time, you'll notice an improvement in your ability to concentrate, manage stress, and make thoughtful decisions, all of which fuel your ambition.

Emotional Resilience

Pursuing ambitious goals often comes with setbacks, uncertainty, and stress. Without self-care, these challenges can quickly become overwhelming, leading to burnout and loss of motivation. Self-care gives you the emotional strength to handle these challenges, allowing you to face them with a sense of balance and resilience.

Regularly checking in with yourself, processing emotions, and taking breaks when needed helps you build the emotional fortitude to bounce back from difficulties. It also prevents you from becoming emotionally reactive, enabling you to respond to challenges with greater clarity and poise. This emotional resilience allows you to stay connected to your goals, even when the path forward isn't easy.

Practical Insight: Develop an emotional check-in routine where you ask yourself how you're feeling, why you're feeling that way, and what you need to support yourself. This practice helps you acknowledge your emotions without judgment, making it easier to manage stress and stay motivated.

Creativity and Innovation

Many of the greatest breakthroughs come during moments of rest or relaxation. When you're constantly pushing yourself, you leave little room for creative thinking. Taking time for self-care allows your mind to wander, explore new ideas, and make connections you wouldn't see when you're in "go mode" all the time.

164

Think about how often you've come up with your best ideas while taking a shower, going for a walk, or simply letting your mind drift. These moments of downtime give your brain the opportunity to process information, connect the dots, and generate innovative solutions. By stepping away from the grind, you create space for creativity to flourish.

Practical Insight: Schedule regular "white space" into your calendar—time where you're not focused on a specific task or goal. Whether it's a weekend hike, a hobby you enjoy, or simply sitting in silence, these moments of relaxation are where inspiration often strikes.

The Self-Care Advantage

By integrating self-care into your routine, you're not just preventing burnout—you're actively fueling your ambition. Self-care equips you with the physical energy, mental clarity, emotional resilience, and creative insight needed to pursue your goals with passion and purpose. It transforms your approach from one of relentless striving to one of sustainable success, allowing you to stay engaged, inspired, and motivated for the long haul.

Remember, self-care isn't a sign of weakness or a luxury reserved for when you've "earned" it. It's a strategic investment in your ability to achieve greatness. By nurturing yourself, you're creating a solid foundation that supports your ambitions, ensuring that you can continue to chase your dreams with vitality, enthusiasm, and unwavering resolve.

Creating a Balanced Daily Routine

Balancing ambition with self-care starts with how you structure your day. A balanced daily routine allows you to pursue your goals while ensuring you're taking time for rest, reflection, and rejuvenation. The key is intentionality—creating a routine that supports both your ambitions and your well-being, so you're not just productive but also fulfilled and energized.

Here's a framework for designing a balanced daily routine:

Prioritize Sleep

Sleep is non-negotiable when it comes to maintaining high levels of energy, focus, and emotional resilience. Studies consistently show that adequate sleep improves memory, decision-making, and emotional regulation—all essential for success. Yet, sleep is often the first thing we sacrifice when we're busy or stressed.

Practical Insights: Aim for 7–9 hours of sleep each night. Create a bedtime routine that signals to your body that it's time to wind down, such as dimming the lights, reading a book, or listening to calming music. Avoid screens at least 30 minutes before bed, as the blue light can interfere with your ability to fall asleep. Consider setting an alarm not just for waking up, but also for when you need to start winding down for the night. By prioritizing sleep, you're investing in the energy and mental clarity you need to tackle your ambitions with vigor.

Morning Mindfulness

How you start your day sets the tone for everything that follows. Instead of jumping straight into emails, to-do lists, or social media, take a few minutes for mindfulness or meditation. This simple practice helps you center yourself, set intentions, and approach the day clearly and calmly. Even just five minutes of mindful breathing, journaling, or expressing gratitude can create a positive mindset that carries through the rest of your day.

Practical Insights: Choose a practice that resonates with you, whether it's deep breathing, a short guided meditation, or writing down three things you're grateful for. If mornings are hectic, try practicing mindfulness while brushing your teeth, drinking your coffee, or during your commute. These small moments of stillness will help ground you and provide a sense of direction before the day's demands begin.

Breaks Throughout the Day

The pressure to stay constantly productive can be overwhelming, but research shows that taking regular breaks actually enhances focus and efficiency. Stepping away from your tasks, even for a few minutes, allows your brain to rest and recharge, preventing mental fatigue and burnout.[49]

Practical Insights: Use the "Pomodoro Technique," which involves working for 25 minutes and then taking a 5-minute break. During these breaks, engage in activities that help you decompress— step outside for fresh air, stretch your body, drink a glass of water, or practice deep breathing. For longer breaks, consider taking a walk, listening to music, or chatting with a friend. These pauses will refresh your mind and increase your overall productivity.[50]

Physical Activity

Incorporating movement into your daily routine boosts energy, enhances mood, and sharpens mental clarity. Physical activity isn't just about staying fit; it's a powerful way to relieve stress, improve cognitive function, and maintain the stamina needed to pursue your ambitions.

Practical Insights: Find an activity that you enjoy, whether it's a morning jog, yoga, dancing, or an evening walk. If your schedule is tight, try incorporating movement into your day by taking the stairs, doing desk stretches, or setting a timer to remind yourself to stand up every hour. Consistency is key, so aim for at least 20–30 minutes of activity most days of the week. Remember, even small bursts of movement can have a big impact on your energy and focus.

Healthy Boundaries

In today's hyper-connected world, it's easy for work to bleed into every aspect of your life, making it feel impossible to truly disconnect. However, setting healthy boundaries around your work time is crucial for maintaining a sense of balance and ensuring you have time for self-care and personal interests.

Practical Insights: Define your work hours and stick to them as much as possible. Communicate your boundaries to colleagues, such as not answering emails after a certain time or turning off work notifications during your personal time. If you work from home, designate a specific workspace to create a mental separation between work and relaxation. This helps prevent burnout and allows you to fully recharge, making you more effective when you're on the clock.

End-of-Day Reflection

Taking a few moments at the end of each day to reflect on what went well, what challenges you faced, and how you felt is a powerful way to process your experiences and release any lingering stress. This practice helps you identify patterns, celebrate small wins, and gain insights into areas where you can improve.

Practical Insights: Set aside 5–10 minutes to journal or meditate on your day's events. Ask yourself questions like: *"What am I proud of today?" "What challenges did I face?" "How did I handle them?"* and *"What can I do differently tomorrow?"* This simple habit fosters self-awareness, encourages gratitude, and reinforces a growth mindset, all of which contribute to a more balanced and intentional life.

Putting It All Together

Creating a balanced daily routine isn't about rigidly following a set schedule—it's about finding what works for you and being intentional about how you spend your time. Start by incorporating one or two of these practices into your day and gradually build from there. Remember, balance is a journey, not a destination. There will be days when things don't go as planned, and that's okay. The goal is to create a routine that nurtures both your ambition and your well-being, allowing you to pursue your goals with energy, focus, and joy.

By integrating self-care into your daily routine, you're not just setting yourself up for success; you're ensuring that your pursuit of your goals remains sustainable, fulfilling, and aligned with your overall well-being.

Setting Boundaries Without Guilt

One of the most common obstacles to balancing ambition with self-care is guilt. Many ambitious people feel guilty when they take time for themselves, worrying that they should be working harder, pushing further, or doing more. This guilt often stems from societal pressures or internal beliefs that equate constant busyness with worthiness or success. But self-care is not selfish—it's essential for long-term success. By setting boundaries, you're not only protecting your energy but also ensuring that you can show up fully for the things that matter most.

Here's how to set boundaries without guilt:

Reframe Self-Care as Necessary

Instead of viewing self-care as an indulgence, recognize that it's a crucial part of your success strategy. You wouldn't expect a car to run on empty, and you can't expect yourself to function at your best if you're depleted. Just as athletes need rest days to perform at their peak, you need moments of rest and recovery to sustain your drive and ambition.

Practical Insight: The next time you feel guilty about taking a break, remind yourself that self-care is an investment in your future productivity and success. Consider scheduling self-care into your calendar just as you would an important meeting or deadline, treating it as a non-negotiable part of your routine. This shift in perspective reinforces the idea that taking care of yourself is not a distraction from your goals but a critical part of achieving them.

Communicate Your Boundaries

Let the people around you—colleagues, friends, family—know when you need time for yourself. Whether it's setting work boundaries, protecting your personal time, or carving out space for hobbies, clear communication helps avoid misunderstandings and reinforces that your self-care is non-negotiable. Often, people respect your boundaries more than you expect; they just need to understand them.

Practical Insight: Start by clearly stating your needs in a calm and assertive manner. For example, if you need uninterrupted time to focus on a project, let your colleagues know that you'll be unavailable for calls or emails during certain hours. Or if you've set aside time for family or personal activities, communicate this to ensure that others know when you're not to be disturbed. Remember, setting boundaries is about respecting your time and energy, not about pushing others away.

Practice Saying "No"

Ambition often comes with a tendency to say "yes" to every opportunity, project, or request, out of fear of missing out or disappointing others. However, saying yes to everything can lead to overwhelm, stress, and burnout. Learning to say "no" is an essential skill for protecting your time and energy. Saying no to what doesn't serve you creates space for what truly matters.

Practical Insight: When faced with a new opportunity or request, pause and ask yourself, *"Does this align with my current goals and priorities?"* If the answer is no, practice responding with kindness and firmness. You don't need to provide an elaborate explanation—sometimes a simple, "I'm unable to take this on right now" is enough.

Let Go of Perfectionism

Perfectionism can make it hard to set boundaries because you feel like everything must be done flawlessly before you can rest. The desire to be perfect often leads to overworking, anxiety, and a fear of letting others down. But the pursuit of perfection is an endless cycle that drains your energy and prevents you from fully enjoying your achievements.

Practical Insight: Instead of aiming for perfection, aim for progress. Recognize that done is often better than perfect and that taking breaks or stepping away from a task doesn't mean you're giving up on excellence—it means you're giving yourself the space to recharge and return with fresh eyes and renewed focus.

Final Thoughts: Embracing Boundaries as Acts of Self-Respect

Setting boundaries isn't about building walls or being less ambitious—it's about honoring your limits, valuing your time, and creating the space needed to thrive. When you set boundaries without guilt, you're telling yourself and others that your well-being is a priority and that taking care of yourself is an essential part of achieving your goals. Remember, boundaries aren't barriers to your ambition; they're the guardrails that keep you on a sustainable path toward success.

Action Step: Create Your Self-Care Plan

Balancing ambition with self-care requires intentional planning and a commitment to prioritizing your well-being. This action step will guide you in creating a personalized self-care plan that aligns with your goals, ensuring that you nurture yourself while pursuing your ambitions. Your self-care plan will serve as a reminder that taking care of yourself is not a distraction but an essential foundation for sustained success.

1. Identify Your Needs: Take a moment to reflect on what you need to feel balanced, energized, and fulfilled. Consider the different areas of your life—physical, mental, emotional, and social—and identify where you might be neglecting your well-being. Ask yourself:

- Do you need more sleep, exercise, or time outdoors?

- Are you craving moments of solitude, relaxation, or creative expression?

- Is there an area where you feel drained or overcommitted?

2. Set Daily and Weekly Self-Care Goals: Based on your identified needs, set small, manageable self-care goals that you can incorporate into your routine. These goals should be realistic, actionable, and tailored to fit your lifestyle. For example:

- Daily: Meditate for 5–10 minutes each morning, take a 10-minute walk during lunch, or set aside 15 minutes to read a book.

- Weekly: Schedule a workout session, dedicate an hour to a hobby, or plan a technology-free evening.

3. Track Your Progress: Keep track of your self-care habits in a journal or planner. Noting how these practices affect your mood, energy, and productivity will help you see the positive impact of prioritizing self-care. This process also allows you to adjust your plan as needed to maintain a healthy balance.

4. Commit to Boundaries: Choose one boundary you need to set this week to protect your self-care time. This could be:

- Turning off work notifications after 7 p.m.

- Saying "no" to a non-essential meeting or task

- Taking a full lunch break without distractions

By setting and respecting your boundaries, you reinforce that your self-care is non-negotiable and vital for sustaining your ambition.

5. Celebrate Your Wins: As you progress with your self-care plan, take time to celebrate your wins, no matter how small. Acknowledge the effort you're putting into nurturing yourself and recognize how these practices are helping you stay balanced, energized, and aligned with your goals.

Ethan in Action: Success Through Balance and Self-Care

As the project progressed, Ethan encountered unexpected challenges that tested his resolve. There were tight deadlines, last-minute changes, and moments when he doubted his ability to succeed without overextending himself. However, each time he felt the urge to push beyond his limits, he reminded himself of his commitment to self-care. Instead of working through lunch or skipping breaks, he took moments to step away, breathe, and recharge. To his surprise, this approach not only preserved his energy but also improved his creativity and problem-solving abilities.

Ethan's decision to prioritize self-care didn't go unnoticed. One afternoon, a colleague approached him, saying, "I've noticed you seem more focused and calm lately, even with all the pressure we're under. How do you manage it?" Ethan smiled, realizing that his journey was not just about his own well-being but also about setting an example for others. "I've learned that taking care of myself doesn't mean I'm any less ambitious," he replied. "In fact, it's the very thing that helps me stay sharp and give my best."

By the end of the project, not only had Ethan successfully led his team to achieve their goals, but he did so without the burnout that had plagued him in the past. For the first time in his career, he felt that he was pursuing his ambitions in a way that honored both his drive and his need for balance. He began to understand that self-care wasn't a distraction from his goals; it was the foundation that made his success sustainable.

Summary: Balancing Ambition with Self-Care

This chapter dismantled the belief that ambition and self-care are incompatible, illustrating how prioritizing self-care actually fuels the drive to achieve your goals. By integrating self-care into your daily routine, you can maintain energy, clarity, and resilience, preventing burnout and enhancing productivity. The chapter guides readers in creating a balanced daily routine, emphasizes the importance of setting healthy boundaries without guilt, and reinforces that self-care is a non-negotiable aspect of sustainable success.

Key Takeaways

- Self-care is a vital part of long-term success and prevents burnout.

- Balancing ambition with self-care leads to improved energy, clarity, and emotional resilience.

- Establishing healthy boundaries ensures you prioritize your well-being while pursuing your goals.

Conclusion: Self-Care as a Foundation for Sustainable Success

Balancing ambition with self-care isn't about choosing one over the other—it's about realizing that they can and should coexist. As we've seen, ignoring self-care in the name of ambition leads to burnout, exhaustion, and a sense of emptiness that undermines even the most significant achievements. But when you make self-care an integral part of your journey, you're not only nurturing your well-being but also laying the foundation for a more sustainable and fulfilling path to success.

By integrating self-care into your daily routine, setting boundaries without guilt, and understanding that rest is a critical component of productivity, you redefine what it means to be ambitious. This new approach allows you to pursue your goals with renewed energy, creativity, and resilience, ensuring that your drive doesn't come at the expense of your health and happiness.

Ultimately, self-care isn't a distraction from your ambition—it's the fuel that sustains it. When you take time to rest, recharge, and honor your needs, you equip yourself to show up more fully, both for your goals and for the people around you. The journey to success doesn't have to be a marathon of exhaustion; it can be a balanced, intentional pursuit where your achievements are enhanced by the well-being that supports them.

As you continue forward, remember that taking care of yourself is not a sign of weakness, but a testament to your strength. It's an acknowledgment that your ambitions are worthy of the best version of you—a version that thrives, not just survives. This balanced approach to ambition and self-care is your gateway to a life of sustained success and genuine fulfillment.

Eight

☙

The Power of Letting Go

Ethan leaned back in his office chair, staring at the glowing cityscape outside his window. Despite the recent success of his latest marketing campaign, a nagging sense of unease weighed him down. He had achieved what he set out to accomplish, but instead of relief, all he felt was tension, like a knot tightening in his chest. He glanced at the calendar on his desk, crammed with back-to-back meetings, deadlines, and new projects. It was as if each achievement only brought more expectations, more pressure to maintain an image of perfection.

The chirp of his phone snapped him back to reality—another meeting request, another task added to his already overwhelming list. Ethan sighed, resisting the urge to toss the phone across the room. He had been down this road before, chasing one success after another, constantly afraid of letting anything slip. But deep down, he knew that *this path, the one that demanded he be in control of every single detail, was unsustainable.*

That evening, Ethan attended a networking event where he ran into Rachel, his colleague who had always seemed to handle the pressures of their industry with remarkable ease. They talked over drinks, and before long, Ethan found himself confiding in her. "I feel like I'm constantly juggling everything, trying to keep it all perfect. But no matter how much I achieve, it's never enough."

Rachel studied him for a moment, then smiled knowingly. "You know, Ethan, maybe the problem isn't about achieving more. Maybe it's about learning to let go of the idea that you need to control everything."

Ethan frowned. "But if I let go, things might fall apart. How do I even know if I'm doing enough?"

"You don't," Rachel said simply. "And that's the point. Real growth doesn't happen when you're clinging to control—it happens when you trust yourself and the process enough to let go."

Ethan pondered her words long after the conversation ended, unable to shake the feeling that she was right. He thought about how tightly he'd been holding onto every detail, how exhausting it was to micromanage every aspect of his life. But letting go? That felt like walking into uncharted territory.

The next morning, Ethan decided to try something different. Instead of overseeing every aspect of his team's project, he chose to delegate more responsibilities, giving them room to make their own decisions. As

181

he handed out tasks, he felt the familiar pang of anxiety creeping in. What if they made mistakes? What if the project didn't meet his high standards? Every instinct urged him to step back in and take control, but Rachel's words echoed in his mind, and he resisted.

As the days passed, Ethan watched his team rise to the occasion. They brought fresh ideas, tackled challenges head-on, and solved problems in ways he hadn't anticipated. By allowing himself to let go, Ethan saw his team's potential unfold, and for the first time in a long while, he felt a flicker of hope. Maybe letting go wasn't about losing control but about creating space for growth.

One evening, as he walked home, Ethan realized he hadn't checked his emails all day—a small victory, but a victory nonetheless. He had trusted his team, and the world hadn't crumbled. Instead, it had expanded, filled with possibilities he'd never seen when he was too busy trying to manage every detail.

But just as Ethan began to embrace this newfound sense of freedom, an important presentation loomed on the horizon, and old habits started creeping back in. He found himself staying up late, tweaking slides, rehearsing his lines, and double-checking every statistic. The fear of imperfection wrapped around him like a familiar blanket, suffocating yet strangely comforting.

The night before the presentation, Ethan's wife found him in his study, surrounded by crumpled papers and empty coffee mugs. "You've been at this for hours," she said softly, placing a hand on his shoulder. "Maybe it's time to let it be."

"I just want it to be perfect," Ethan muttered, not taking his eyes off the screen.

She tilted her head, studying him with that look she always gave when she saw right through him. "But who told you that it needs to be perfect? Maybe it's enough to just be you."

Her words hit him like a splash of cold water. For so long, Ethan had convinced himself that his worth was tied to flawless execution, that any sign of imperfection meant failure. But what if she was right? What if letting go of that need for perfection was the very thing that could set him free?

Taking a deep breath, Ethan closed his laptop. For the first time in weeks, he allowed himself to walk away, knowing that he had done enough.

Introduction: Releasing the Need for Control

Letting go is one of the most challenging, yet liberating, shifts we can make on our journey toward balance. It's a process that asks us to surrender our need for perfection, release the illusion of control, and embrace the uncertainty that life inevitably brings. For many, this can feel like giving up or admitting defeat. However, the power of letting go isn't about abandoning our ambitions or aspirations; it's about making space for what truly matters.

In this chapter, we will explore how surrendering control can lead to deeper connections, greater creativity, and a more authentic experience of success. Letting go is not an act of weakness but one of immense strength. It's the conscious choice to trust ourselves, our journey, and the process of life—even when the path ahead is unclear.

Are you ready to take that leap of faith? To let go of the stories you've told yourself about what it means to be successful and instead open yourself up to the possibilities that come when you surrender? It's time to explore how letting go can become one of the most powerful tools on your journey to finding balance and true success.

Why Letting Go Leads to Growth

When we cling too tightly to specific outcomes, we often become prisoners of our own expectations. We convince ourselves that there's only one path to success, one formula for achieving our goals. But in doing so, we narrow our vision and miss out on the countless opportunities and experiences that lie just beyond our carefully constructed plans. Letting go doesn't mean abandoning our goals; it means allowing ourselves to be open to the unexpected turns and detours that can lead to even greater growth and success.

Letting go is about releasing the illusion of control and embracing the idea that life is unpredictable. It's about trusting that the journey itself holds valuable lessons and opportunities, even when things don't unfold the way we imagined. This shift in mindset creates space for growth in ways we could never have anticipated. Here's how letting go can become a catalyst for profound personal and professional development:

Opens Space for Creativity

When we let go of the need to control every detail, we make room for creativity to flourish. Clinging to rigid plans or expectations limits our thinking, trapping us in a box of what we believe should happen. But when we loosen our grip, we invite fresh perspectives, ideas, and solutions to emerge. The creative process thrives in uncertainty, and some of the most innovative breakthroughs happen when we step back and allow ourselves to explore without fear of failure.

For example, think of artists who let go of the outcome and simply allow the brush to flow across the canvas. They discover new techniques, colors, and forms that wouldn't have been possible if they were fixated on achieving a perfect picture. Similarly, when we approach our goals with an open mind, we often stumble upon solutions and opportunities that are far more imaginative and effective than anything we could have planned.

Reduces Stress and Anxiety

The need to control every outcome can be exhausting. It's a relentless cycle of anxiety, as we constantly worry about whether things will go according to plan. We become so focused on preventing failure that we forget to enjoy the process. By letting go, we shift our focus from rigid control to trust—trusting ourselves, trusting others, and trusting that life will unfold as it's meant to.

When we let go, we experience a profound sense of relief. We no longer feel the need to micromanage every detail or predict every possible scenario. This reduction in stress allows us to approach challenges with a clearer mind and a calmer heart, making us more resilient and capable of navigating whatever comes our way. Instead of being overwhelmed by the pressure to make everything perfect, we learn to embrace the journey, imperfections and all.

Enhances Adaptability

In a world that is constantly changing, adaptability is one of the most valuable skills we can cultivate. When we let go of rigid expectations and the need for everything to go according to plan, we become more agile and responsive to life's changes. Instead of seeing obstacles as threats to our goals, we begin to view them as opportunities to pivot and grow in new directions.

Letting go allows us to be present and attuned to what's happening around us. This heightened awareness enables us to recognize opportunities that might have been invisible when we were fixated on a specific outcome. By being open to change, we develop the flexibility needed to navigate uncertainty with confidence and grace. We begin to understand that success isn't about following a predetermined path—it's about adapting to the twists and turns along the way and finding new ways to move forward.[51]

Fosters Personal Growth and Self-Discovery

When we stop clinging to who we think we should be or what we believe we should achieve, we create space for genuine self-discovery. Letting go encourages us to step outside our comfort zones, confront our fears, and challenge the limiting beliefs that have held us back. As we release the need to control every aspect of our lives, we gain a deeper understanding of ourselves—our strengths, passions, and values.

This process of letting go often leads to profound personal growth, as we learn to accept ourselves for who we are rather than who we think we need to be. We begin to see that our worth isn't tied to our achievements or how closely we adhere to our plans. Instead, it's found in our ability to adapt, learn, and grow from every experience—both the successes and the setbacks.

Cultivates Resilience

Finally, letting go teaches us resilience. When we release the need to control every outcome, we become more comfortable with uncertainty and more capable of bouncing back from setbacks. We learn that failure isn't the end—it's simply a part of the journey. This realization strengthens our ability to persevere, even when things don't go as planned.

By letting go, we develop a mindset that sees challenges as opportunities for growth rather than threats to our success. We become less afraid of taking risks because we understand that we have the ability to adapt and learn from whatever comes our way. This resilience not only helps us overcome obstacles but also propels us toward greater achievements, as we're no longer held back by the fear of failure.

The Freedom in Letting Go

When we learn to let go, we discover a sense of freedom that allows us to move forward with greater confidence, creativity, and clarity. We begin to understand that the path to growth isn't always a straight line— it's a journey filled with unexpected twists, turns, and opportunities to evolve. By releasing our need for control, we open ourselves to the infinite possibilities that life has to offer, and in doing so, we unlock our true potential.

Letting go doesn't mean giving up—it means making room for growth, allowing ourselves to be guided by the flow of life, and trusting that even when things don't go as planned, we are still moving forward. This is the essence of true growth: the willingness to surrender to the unknown and embrace the beauty of the journey.

Letting Go of Perfectionism

One of the hardest things to let go of is the relentless need for perfection. Perfectionism whispers in our ear, promising that if we just work a little harder, refine a little more, or wait a little longer, we'll achieve flawless results. It convinces us that anything less than perfect isn't worth pursuing, and that our value is tied to how seamlessly we can present ourselves and our work to the world. But perfectionism is a trap—an illusion that keeps us from taking action, stifles our creativity, and prevents us from reaching our true potential.

The pursuit of perfection can be paralyzing. We spend countless hours obsessing over details, revising, and second-guessing every decision, convinced that we're just one step away from getting it "right." But in reality, perfection is an ever-moving target, always just out of reach. No matter how much we achieve, there's always another flaw to fix, another adjustment to make. This endless chase leads to burnout, frustration, and often a sense of inadequacy, no matter how much we accomplish.

Embracing Progress Over Perfection

While a whole chapter is devoted to embracing imperfection later in the book, touching on it here is important. Letting go of perfectionism means shifting our focus from flawless execution to consistent progress. It's about recognizing that true growth doesn't happen in the pursuit of perfection but in the willingness to take imperfect action. When we let go of the need for everything to be just right, we open ourselves up to possibilities, insights, and opportunities for learning that we would otherwise miss.[52]

Instead of obsessing over every detail, ask yourself: *"Is this good enough to move forward?"* Accept that there will always be room for improvement, but that doesn't mean you have to wait until everything is perfect to take the next step. By prioritizing progress, you give yourself permission to experiment, learn from your mistakes, and refine your approach along the way.

The Fear Behind Perfectionism

At the heart of perfectionism lies fear—the fear of failure, judgment, or not being enough. We worry that if we present anything less than perfect, we'll be exposed, criticized, or rejected. But this fear is often what holds us back from achieving our goals. It keeps us playing small, unwilling to take risks or step outside our comfort zone.

However, when we let go of the need to be perfect, we begin to realize that mistakes are not signs of failure but stepping stones to growth. They provide valuable feedback, teaching us what works, what doesn't, and how we can improve. Instead of seeing mistakes as proof of inadequacy, we start to view them as opportunities to adapt, learn, and evolve. This mindset shift allows us to take more chances, pursue our goals with greater courage, and ultimately achieve more than we ever thought possible.

Finding Freedom in Imperfection

When we release the need for perfection, we free ourselves from the weight of unrealistic expectations. We begin to see that life is not about achieving a flawless state but about embracing our journey—messy, unpredictable, and full of surprises. This freedom allows us to take action even when we don't have all the answers, to try new things without fear of falling short, and to celebrate our progress, no matter how small.

Embracing imperfection means accepting that we are human, that growth is a process, and that the value of our work lies not in its flawlessness but in the authenticity and effort we bring to it. It's in those moments of vulnerability, when we allow ourselves to be seen as we are—imperfect but striving—that we connect most deeply with others and experience the greatest growth.

Practical Steps to Letting Go of Perfectionism

1. Set Realistic Goals: Perfectionists often set goals that are unachievable or overly ambitious, leading to frustration and burnout. Start by setting realistic, attainable goals that focus on progress rather than perfection. Break tasks into smaller steps and celebrate each milestone along the way, no matter how minor it may seem.

2. Adopt a "Good Enough" Mindset: Challenge yourself to identify when something is "good enough" to move forward. This doesn't mean settling for mediocrity; it means recognizing when your work

meets the necessary standards and resisting the urge to over-refine. Remember, done is often better than perfect.

3. Embrace Mistakes as Learning Opportunities: Instead of viewing mistakes as failures, see them as valuable feedback. Each misstep is an opportunity to learn, adjust, and grow. Ask yourself, *"What can I learn from this experience?"* and use it as a stepping stone to move forward with more knowledge and confidence.

4. Celebrate Effort, Not Just Outcomes: Perfectionists tend to focus on the end result, but growth happens in the effort and process. Take time to acknowledge your hard work, dedication, and the progress you've made, regardless of the final outcome. This shift in focus helps you appreciate your journey and reinforces the value of perseverance.

5. Practice Self-Compassion: Be kind to yourself when things don't go as planned. Instead of harshly criticizing your mistakes, treat yourself with the same understanding and encouragement you would offer a friend. Self-compassion helps to quiet the inner critic and fosters a more supportive environment for growth.

The Path Forward

Letting go of perfectionism isn't about lowering your standards or giving up on excellence—it's about recognizing that true excellence lies in the willingness to take risks, make mistakes, and grow along the way. When you release the unrealistic expectation of perfection, you gain the freedom to explore, experiment, and evolve without the fear of falling short.

By embracing imperfection, you not only open yourself up to greater creativity and adaptability but also allow yourself to experience the richness and beauty of life's journey. You discover that it's not about reaching an ideal state of flawlessness, but about showing up as you are, doing your best, and finding fulfillment in the process. After all, it's through our imperfections that we learn, connect, and ultimately, grow.

Action Step: Practicing Surrender

Letting go is a skill that requires practice, especially if you've spent much of your life striving for control or perfection. This week, take intentional steps to release your grip on situations, tasks, or expectations that are causing you stress or holding you back. Here's a step-by-step guide to help you practice the art of surrender:

1. **Identify an Area of Control:** Choose one specific area of your life where you feel the need to be in constant control or where you're struggling with perfectionism. It could be a project at work, a personal goal, a relationship, or even how you manage your daily schedule.

2. **Set a "Good Enough" Goal:** Instead of aiming for perfection, set a goal that's "good enough" for this task or situation. Define what a satisfactory outcome looks like—not perfect, but effective and

complete. This helps you shift your focus from flawless execution to meaningful progress.

3. **Delegate or Release One Task:** Choose one task or responsibility within this area that you can delegate to someone else or simply let go of. Allow yourself to step back, trusting that things will unfold without your constant involvement. Observe how this makes you feel—whether it brings relief, anxiety, or something in between. Resist the urge to jump back in and fix or control the outcome.

4. **Embrace Mistakes and Learning:** Throughout the week, notice any mistakes or imperfections that arise in this process. Instead of seeing them as failures, write them down and reflect on what you've learned from each one. How did this experience help you grow? What insights did you gain by letting go of control?

5. **Practice a Daily "Letting Go" Meditation:** Set aside 5–10 minutes each day to practice a simple meditation focused on surrender. Sit in a comfortable position, close your eyes, and take a few deep breaths. As you inhale, silently repeat the phrase "I let go," and as you exhale, release any tension or worry you're holding onto. Allow yourself to feel the weight lifting as you practice this intentional act of letting go.

6. **Reflect on Your Experience:** At the end of the week, take some time to journal about your experience. Ask yourself:

   • What did you learn about yourself by letting go?

- How did it impact your stress levels, creativity, or productivity?

- Were there any unexpected positive outcomes that emerged from releasing control?

Ethan in Action: Surrendering to the Moment

The day following the conversation with his wife, Ethan stood before his audience, heart pounding in his chest. *As he began his presentation, he felt the familiar flutter of nerves but chose not to fight them. He didn't focus on delivering every word flawlessly or impressing everyone in the room. Instead, he let himself be present, speaking from a place of authenticity. And as he looked into the faces of his audience, something shifted. They weren't just seeing a polished executive—they were seeing him, imperfections and all.*

When he finished, the applause was louder than he'd expected, but more than that, it felt genuine. Ethan realized it wasn't just about the success of the presentation. It was about the fact that, for once, he had let go of his need to be perfect. He had shown up as himself, and that had been more than enough.

In the weeks that followed, Ethan continued to practice letting go, though it wasn't always easy. There were days when the urge to control crept back in, when the fear of failure made him question whether he was doing enough. But each time, he reminded himself of what Rachel had said—that real growth happened not when he held on but when he allowed himself to release.

With each step, Ethan discovered something unexpected: the more he let go, the more he gained. His work became more creative, his relationships more authentic, and his life fuller in ways he hadn't imagined. In letting go of the need to control everything, Ethan found a sense of freedom he never thought possible—the freedom to be himself, to embrace imperfection, and to find peace in the journey, not just the destination.

Summary: The Power of Letting Go

In this chapter, we explored the transformative impact of letting go and how surrendering control can lead to deeper personal growth, creativity, and a more authentic experience of success. Additionally, we dove deeper into why letting go is crucial for growth.

The chapter highlights how clinging to control narrows our vision, limits creativity, and generates stress, while letting go opens us up to new possibilities, enhances adaptability, fosters resilience, and leads to genuine self-discovery.

Key Takeaways

- Letting go is not about giving up; it's about making space for growth, creativity, and authentic experiences by releasing the need for control and perfection.

- Trusting the process allows us to be more adaptable, resilient, and open to new opportunities, leading to greater personal and professional growth.

- Embracing progress over perfection helps us overcome the fear of failure and encourages us to take action, experiment, and learn from our experiences.

Conclusion: Embracing the Power of Letting Go

Letting go isn't about giving up on your goals or abandoning your ambitions. It's about easing up on the relentless grip we often have on life, work, and ourselves. In this chapter, we explored how stepping back from the need to control everything can be one of the most liberating and transformative shifts we can make. When we're not so focused on achieving a flawless outcome, we start to see possibilities, opportunities, and paths that we'd otherwise miss.

It's easy to get trapped in the pursuit of perfection, thinking that if we just push harder, plan more, or control every little detail, we'll somehow get everything right. But that mindset often leaves us stuck, stressed, and too afraid to take risks. Letting go allows us to be more flexible, to adapt, to make mistakes, and—most importantly—to learn. It's in those moments of uncertainty and imperfection that real creativity and growth often emerge.

Life is unpredictable, and that's okay. By loosening our grip, we create space to breathe, experiment, and discover new ways of approaching challenges. In that space, we often find a sense of freedom, resilience, and authenticity that rigid control could never provide.

As you move forward, consider where you can let go a little more— whether it's easing up on your own expectations, trusting others to take the lead, or simply allowing yourself to make a few mistakes along the way. The journey doesn't need to be perfect; it just needs to be yours.

And sometimes, the most beautiful things happen when we're willing to let them unfold naturally.

Nine

✿

Cultivating Gratitude Along the Journey

Ethan sat at his desk, the flicker of his computer screen illuminating the dimly lit room. *It had been another long day filled with meetings, deadlines, and endless to-do lists. Despite his recent successes, he felt an all-too-familiar sense of emptiness creeping in, as if each achievement was just another item to check off a never-ending list. He rubbed his tired eyes, wondering how he'd ended up here once again— trapped in the cycle of hustle he had vowed to leave behind.*

One evening, as he walked home in the cool twilight, something caught his eye. It was the sight of an elderly man sitting on a park bench, his face lit up with a serene smile as he fed a flock of birds. For a moment, Ethan felt a pang of envy. How could someone find such contentment in a seemingly mundane moment? As he paused to watch, he felt a sudden urge to reconnect with the simple joys he'd been neglecting.

Inspired, Ethan decided to start a small experiment that evening. He pulled out an old notebook and began to jot down three things he was grateful for that day. At first, the task felt awkward, almost forced—after all, gratitude wasn't something that came naturally in the midst of his busy routine. But as the days turned into weeks, he found himself noticing more of the small moments that brought him joy: the warmth of his morning coffee, a smile from a stranger, the support of his team during a challenging project.

Introduction: Gratitude as a Daily Practice

Gratitude is more than just a fleeting emotion or a polite "thank you"—it's a powerful, intentional practice that can reshape how we experience our journey toward success. In a world that often emphasizes what's missing or what's next, gratitude serves as a reminder of the abundance that already exists in our lives. It shifts our focus from the relentless pursuit of more to an appreciation for the present moment, grounding us in a sense of contentment and fulfillment, even as we continue to strive for our goals.

Research has shown that gratitude can have profound effects on our mental health, resilience, and overall well-being. It rewires our brains to recognize the positive aspects of our lives, helping us build a mindset that isn't driven by scarcity or lack, but by appreciation and abundance. When practiced consistently, gratitude becomes a stabilizing force, one that helps us navigate challenges with grace and respond to setbacks with a renewed sense of purpose.[53]

In this chapter, we'll explore the transformative power of gratitude and how it can serve as a fuel for your ambitions rather than a distraction from them. You'll discover that gratitude is not about ignoring your goals or settling for less, but about enriching your journey by celebrating the progress you've made and the experiences you've gained along the way. We'll explore practical techniques to weave gratitude into your daily routine, turning it from an occasional thought into a guiding principle that nurtures both your inner peace and external success.

As you read on, you'll see that gratitude isn't just an occasional practice—it's a mindset, a lens through which you can view your life, and a powerful tool that can elevate your path toward success. By embracing gratitude, you'll find that your journey becomes more meaningful, your achievements more fulfilling, and your sense of peace more enduring.

How Gratitude Shifts Your Mindset

Gratitude is a powerful tool that shifts your mindset from scarcity to abundance. It invites you to focus not on what you lack or what you have yet to accomplish, but on the richness and blessings that already exist in your life. This doesn't mean you should abandon your goals or aspirations; instead, it means appreciating the progress you've made, the lessons you've learned, and the experiences you've gained along the way. By recognizing the value of the present moment, gratitude allows you to approach your ambitions from a place of wholeness and fulfillment, rather than from a sense of deficiency or constant striving.

Gratitude has the unique ability to transform your perspective, infusing your journey with a sense of purpose, connection, and joy. When you cultivate a habit of gratitude, you start to see opportunities where others see obstacles, strengths where others see weaknesses, and abundance where others see scarcity. This shift is not just a change in attitude—it's a fundamental reorientation of how you engage with the world around you. Here's how gratitude can significantly enhance your pursuit of success:

Boosts Emotional Well-Being

Gratitude has been scientifically proven to increase feelings of happiness, contentment, and overall life satisfaction. When you regularly practice gratitude, you train your brain to notice the positive aspects of your life, which creates a ripple effect of emotional abundance. This shift in focus helps reduce stress and anxiety, allowing you to approach your goals with greater enthusiasm and optimism. Instead of dwelling on setbacks or obstacles, gratitude helps you celebrate your wins, no matter how small, fueling your motivation and keeping you energized for the journey ahead.

When you take time each day to reflect on what went well, even during challenging times, you reinforce a mindset that recognizes growth and progress rather than dwelling on perceived shortcomings. This enhanced emotional well-being becomes a foundation from which you can pursue your ambitions with clarity and resilience.

Strengthens Resilience

Life is full of challenges, and the path to success is often marked by setbacks, failures, and unexpected obstacles. Gratitude acts as a buffer during these tough times, helping you maintain perspective and find meaning even in adversity. By consciously focusing on what you're grateful for—whether it's the support of a colleague, a lesson learned from a mistake, or simply the strength to keep moving forward—you cultivate resilience. Gratitude reminds you that even in the face of difficulty, there are still aspects of your life that are worth appreciating, which gives you the strength to persevere.

For instance, when you encounter a setback at work, shifting your focus to the skills you've developed, the people who have supported you, or the progress you've made so far can prevent you from getting discouraged. This resilience enables you to bounce back from challenges with a renewed sense of purpose rather than allowing them to derail your journey.

Enhances Relationships

Gratitude is a bridge that connects us to others. When you express genuine appreciation for the people around you—be it colleagues, friends, or family—you strengthen those relationships by creating a sense of mutual respect and trust. Gratitude fosters empathy and compassion, making others feel valued and seen, which in turn encourages deeper and more meaningful connections. These connections are vital for both personal growth and professional success, as they create a support network that can help you navigate life's challenges and celebrate your achievements.

Imagine expressing appreciation to a coworker who helped you with a project or taking a moment to thank a friend for their unwavering support. Such acts of gratitude not only nurture your relationships but also cultivate an environment of positivity and collaboration, which can be a powerful catalyst for collective success.

Shifts Your Focus from "Have To" to "Get To"

One of the most transformative aspects of gratitude is how it reframes your daily experiences. Instead of approaching tasks with a mindset of obligation ("I have to do this"), gratitude encourages you to see them as opportunities ("I get to do this"). This subtle but powerful shift changes how you engage with your responsibilities and goals. You begin to view challenges as chances to learn and grow, and mundane tasks become opportunities to contribute, connect, or develop your skills. This shift not only increases your overall satisfaction but also helps you approach your work with greater enthusiasm and energy.

For example, instead of dreading a long meeting, you might find yourself feeling grateful for the chance to share your ideas, collaborate with others, or learn something new. This mindset change transforms everyday experiences into moments of possibility and growth.

Amplifies Your Sense of Purpose

When you cultivate gratitude, you start to see the bigger picture and the interconnectedness of your journey. Instead of focusing solely on the end result, gratitude helps you appreciate the steps along the way—the people who have supported you, the skills you've acquired, and the experiences that have shaped you. This awareness amplifies your sense of purpose, reminding you that every part of your journey has value. As a result, you're more likely to stay motivated and committed, even when the road gets tough.

By acknowledging the contributions of others, the resources available to you, and the progress you've made, gratitude deepens your sense of purpose and reinforces your belief that your efforts are meaningful. This sense of purpose fuels your drive to keep moving forward, no matter what challenges arise.

Daily Gratitude Practices

Gratitude is more than a one-time action; it's a habit that, when nurtured, can profoundly impact your mindset and overall well-being. Just as you might train your body through regular exercise, cultivating gratitude requires consistent, intentional practice. By incorporating gratitude into your daily routine, you gradually shift your focus toward abundance and positivity, making it a natural part of how you experience the world. Here are some powerful ways to build gratitude into your life:

Gratitude Journaling

Set aside a few moments each day—preferably in the morning or before bed—to write down three things you're grateful for. These can be as simple as a delicious meal, a moment of laughter, or the support of a loved one. You might also reflect on bigger aspects of your life, such as your personal growth, career progress, or the health you enjoy. As you journal, try to be specific and detailed about why you feel grateful. For example, instead of just writing *"I'm grateful for my friend,"* you could write, *"I'm grateful for my friend who called me today to check in—it made me feel supported and valued."* This added depth helps you connect more deeply with the feeling of gratitude.

Practical Insight: Keep your gratitude journal by your bed or in a place you see daily. By making it part of your morning or evening routine, you're more likely to stick with the practice and experience its transformative effects.

Why It Works: Gratitude journaling trains your mind to actively seek out positive experiences, even on challenging days. Over time, this practice rewires your brain to focus more on abundance and less on scarcity, making you more resilient and optimistic. It also creates a written record of the good in your life, which you can revisit whenever you need a boost of positivity.

Gratitude Meditation

Begin or end your day with a few minutes of gratitude meditation. Find a quiet space where you can sit comfortably without distractions. Close your eyes and take a few deep breaths, allowing your body and mind to relax. As you breathe, bring to mind specific aspects of your life that you're thankful for—perhaps a recent accomplishment, the love of a family member, or the beauty of nature around you. Focus on one thing at a time, and as you think about it, let the feeling of gratitude fill your heart. Visualize that sense of gratitude spreading throughout your body, warming you from the inside out.

Practical Insight: If you find it challenging to focus during meditation, consider using a guided gratitude meditation app or video.

These can provide structure and help you stay centered on your gratitude practice.

Why It Works: Gratitude meditation helps you cultivate a deeper sense of appreciation by encouraging you to be fully present with your feelings of thankfulness. It slows down your thoughts, allowing you to savor each moment of gratitude and experience it more intensely. This practice can also reduce stress, increase mindfulness, and set a positive tone for your day.

Express Gratitude to Others

One of the most powerful ways to cultivate gratitude is by sharing it with those around you. Make it a habit to express appreciation to the people in your life—whether it's thanking a coworker for their help, acknowledging a friend's support, or simply telling your partner how much you appreciate them. You can express your gratitude through spoken words, written notes, or small gestures. For instance, consider sending a thank-you email to a colleague who made your day easier or leaving a sticky note with a kind message for a loved one. These expressions of gratitude not only brighten someone else's day but also strengthen your relationships and create a ripple effect of positivity.

Practical Insight: Set a goal to express gratitude to at least one person each day. Whether it's in person, through a message, or even in a social media post, this simple act can have a profound impact on your relationships and overall mindset.

Why It Works: When you take the time to express gratitude to others, you reinforce your own sense of appreciation and deepen your connections. Studies have shown that expressing gratitude increases feelings of happiness and satisfaction, both for the giver and the receiver. It fosters a culture of appreciation, which can lead to more positive interactions and a stronger sense of community.[54]

Create a Gratitude Ritual

Incorporate gratitude into your daily routine by establishing a ritual that works for you. This could be a morning gratitude ritual where you take a moment to acknowledge something you're thankful for as soon as you wake up, or an evening ritual where you reflect on the day's positive moments before going to bed. You might also introduce a gratitude practice at mealtime, where you take a moment to express thanks for the food you're about to enjoy or share something you're grateful for with those around you.

Practical Insight: Involve others in your gratitude ritual, such as family members, friends, or coworkers. Sharing gratitude as a group can create a positive atmosphere and encourage a collective appreciation for the good in your lives.

Why It Works: Creating a gratitude ritual helps anchor the practice into your daily life, making it more automatic and habitual. By linking gratitude to an existing routine, such as waking up, eating, or going to bed, you're more likely to stay consistent and build a lasting habit.[55]

Use Gratitude Prompts Throughout the Day

Throughout your day, remind yourself to practice gratitude by using prompts that nudge you toward a grateful mindset. Set reminders on your phone, place sticky notes with gratitude prompts around your workspace, or create visual cues, such as a photo or object that represents something you're thankful for. Whenever you see these prompts, take a moment to pause, breathe, and reflect on something you appreciate in that moment.

Practical Insight: Choose prompts that resonate with you, such as *"What's one thing I'm grateful for right now?"* or *"Who has made a positive impact on my life today?"* These reminders can be especially helpful on tough days when gratitude might not come as easily.

Why It Works: Gratitude prompts serve as gentle reminders to pause and reconnect with a sense of thankfulness, even when you're busy or stressed. They help you stay present and mindful, ensuring that gratitude remains an active part of your daily experience.

Action Step: Establishing Your Daily Gratitude Ritual

Create a gratitude ritual that fits into your daily routine. This could be a morning gratitude journal, an evening reflection, or a midday gratitude break. Start small—just five minutes a day—and notice how it shifts your perspective and mindset over time.

Ethan in Action: A Compass to Fulfillment

Over time, this simple gratitude practice began to shift something within him. *Instead of focusing solely on what he hadn't accomplished or the endless demands of his career, Ethan started to appreciate the journey itself. He felt lighter, more connected to the world around him, and less consumed by the relentless pursuit of success.*

One afternoon, during a particularly stressful meeting, Ethan caught himself slipping back into old habits—rushing, reacting, and striving for perfection. But instead of spiraling into anxiety, he took a deep breath and thought about his gratitude list. It reminded him that there was more to life than the next deadline or the next goal. He realized that his path wasn't just about what he achieved but how he chose to experience it.

In that moment, Ethan understood that gratitude wasn't just a feel-good exercise—it was a compass guiding him back to what truly mattered. And with each step he took on this journey, he discovered that the more he cultivated gratitude, the more fulfilled and at peace he became.

Summary: Cultivating Gratitude Along the Journey

In this chapter, we explored the transformative power of gratitude and how it can enrich our path toward success. We learned that gratitude is more than just an emotion—it's a practice that can shift our mindset from scarcity to abundance, boost emotional well-being, strengthen resilience, enhance relationships, and amplify our sense of purpose. When we focus on what we have instead of what's missing, we cultivate a more positive and fulfilling perspective on life.

The chapter outlined practical daily gratitude practices, such as journaling, meditation, expressing appreciation to others, creating gratitude rituals, and using gratitude prompts. These practices help reinforce a mindset of thankfulness, making gratitude an integral part of how we experience the world. By establishing a daily gratitude ritual, we can actively shape our journey to be more meaningful, joyful, and aligned with our true values.

Key Takeways

- **Gratitude Shifts Your Mindset:** Practicing gratitude transforms your outlook from scarcity to abundance, allowing you to appreciate your progress, the present moment, and the opportunities in your life, which leads to greater emotional well-being and resilience.

- **Strengthens Relationships and Purpose:** Expressing gratitude deepens your connections with others, fostering empathy and appreciation, while also reinforcing your sense of purpose and commitment to your journey.

- **Gratitude is a Transformative Habit:** By integrating daily gratitude practices like journaling, meditation, and expressing appreciation, you can cultivate a consistent mindset of thankfulness that guides you toward a more balanced and fulfilling path to success.

Conclusion: Gratitude as Fuel for Success

Gratitude is more than a momentary expression; it's a powerful, transformative force that shapes how we navigate life's challenges and achievements. When you choose to focus on gratitude, you're not just acknowledging the good in your life—you're cultivating a mindset that sees possibilities, growth, and abundance. This shift allows you to pursue your ambitions with a sense of fulfillment and resilience, rather than being consumed by stress or the endless pursuit of "more."

By integrating gratitude into your own life, you create a foundation of peace, connection, and purpose that sustains you on your journey. The path to success doesn't have to be marked by burnout or emptiness; it can be fueled by gratitude, leading you to a more balanced, enriching, and rewarding experience.

Let gratitude be your guide and watch as it transforms not only your mindset but also the quality of your journey toward lasting success.

Ten

✿

Embracing Imperfection

Ethan sat in his office, staring at the latest draft of a presentation he'd been working on for weeks. *Despite his best efforts, it didn't feel quite right. He shifted in his chair, his inner critic's voice growing louder with every moment. "This isn't good enough," it whispered, "You need to fix this before anyone sees it." Ethan had always prided himself on his attention to detail and the desire to get things just right, but lately, he was beginning to recognize that this perfectionism was more of a prison than a strength.*

The weight of constant striving for flawlessness had started to take its toll, affecting his work, relationships, and overall sense of happiness. He remembered a recent conversation with his mentor, who had gently reminded him that perfection wasn't the goal—progress was. "Perfectionism is just fear dressed up in fancy clothes," his mentor had said. "It keeps you safe from criticism but also holds you back from growth."

216

Ethan decided it was time to let go of the unrealistic expectations he had placed on himself. As he took a deep breath, he acknowledged the messy, imperfect process that led him here. He knew he needed to embrace his imperfections, not as flaws to be fixed but as essential parts of his journey toward growth and self-acceptance.

Introduction: The Beauty of Imperfection

Perfectionism is often disguised as a noble pursuit, promising us that if we just try a little harder, work a little longer, or fix every flaw, we'll finally be worthy of success. Yet, this relentless drive for flawlessness can be one of the greatest barriers to achieving true fulfillment. The reality is that perfectionism isn't about striving to be the best version of ourselves; it's about avoiding failure, criticism, or vulnerability. It convinces us that anything less than perfect is a failure, that mistakes are unforgivable, and that our worth is tied to how flawless we appear to the world.

The problem with this mindset is that perfection is not only unattainable—it's paralyzing. It keeps us trapped in a cycle of self-doubt, preventing us from taking the very risks that lead to growth and innovation. We delay projects because they're not "ready," hold back our ideas because they're not "good enough," and miss out on opportunities to learn because we're afraid of making mistakes. In our pursuit of perfection, we lose sight of one fundamental truth: it's our imperfections that make us human, relatable, and ultimately, more resilient.

In this chapter, we'll explore the power of embracing imperfection and why letting go of the need to be flawless can lead to more authentic, meaningful success. We'll continue to explore growth as a process, not a destination, and that true progress often comes from the moments when we stumble, learn, and adapt. By shifting your perspective, you'll begin to see that imperfections are not signs of failure but evidence that you are actively engaged in your journey—constantly evolving, learning, and becoming.

As you read on, you'll discover practical tools for challenging your perfectionist tendencies and learn to appreciate the beauty of progress, no matter how messy it may seem. This journey won't be about lowering your standards or settling for mediocrity. Instead, it's about finding peace in your imperfections, celebrating your unique path, and allowing yourself the grace to be a work in progress. Because in the end, it's not perfection that defines us—it's the courage to keep moving forward, one imperfect step at a time.

The Trap of Perfectionism

Perfectionism often disguises itself as a desire for excellence, but beneath its polished surface lies a deeper struggle—a fear of failure, rejection, and a longing for external validation. We convince ourselves that if we can just be perfect—flawless in our work, impeccable in our relationships, or polished in our appearance—we will finally feel worthy, loved, and successful. However, this pursuit of perfection is a moving target, always just out of reach. No matter how hard we try or how much we accomplish, there's always something that could be better, something that isn't quite "enough."

The trap of perfectionism is that it keeps us in a perpetual state of "almost there," never allowing us to feel truly satisfied or at peace with ourselves. Instead of celebrating our progress, we fixate on what's missing or imperfect, constantly raising the bar until even our greatest achievements feel like failures. This mindset doesn't just hinder our ability to grow; it robs us of the joy that comes from being present, taking risks, and engaging fully with life's experiences.

Perfectionism paralyzes us, making it difficult to take action or make decisions. We hesitate to start projects, fearing they won't meet our impossibly high standards. We shy away from opportunities that challenge us because we worry about falling short. When we do take action, we often find ourselves caught in a cycle of overthinking, second-guessing, and endless revisions. Instead of seeing our efforts as valuable steps toward growth, we view them as evidence of our inadequacy.

Yet, the truth is that perfectionism is an illusion. It's a self-imposed barrier that prevents us from fully embracing our potential and living authentically. By clinging to the idea of being perfect, we deny ourselves the freedom to experiment, learn, and evolve. We miss out on the magic that comes from stepping outside our comfort zones, making mistakes, and discovering new strengths along the way.

Embracing imperfection is about recognizing that growth doesn't come from getting everything right the first time; it comes from trying, failing, adjusting, and trying again. It's in our moments of vulnerability, when we dare to show up as we are—flaws and all—that we find the courage to stretch, adapt, and ultimately transform. When we let go of the need to be perfect, we create space for creativity, resilience, and genuine connection with ourselves and others.

By shifting our focus from perfection to progress, we begin to see that our worth isn't tied to flawless execution but to our willingness to show up, take risks, and learn from our experiences. It's in the messy, imperfect moments that we discover who we truly are and what we're capable of achieving. And it's here, in this space of authenticity and growth, that we find the freedom to pursue a life that's not defined by perfection but by the richness of our imperfect journey.

Progress Over Perfection

The key to overcoming perfectionism lies in shifting our focus from achieving flawless outcomes to embracing the beauty of progress. It's easy to fall into the trap of thinking that we need everything to be perfectly aligned before we can begin, but this mindset often leads to stagnation and missed opportunities. The reality is that perfection is a mirage—always on the horizon but never within reach. Instead of striving for an ideal that doesn't exist, we need to recognize that it's the act of moving forward, however imperfectly, that creates true growth and transformation.

Progress is about taking one step at a time, knowing that each step, no matter how small or uncertain, is moving us closer to our goals. When we allow ourselves to take action without the pressure of getting everything right, we create space for learning, experimentation, and discovery. In this mindset, mistakes become valuable lessons, not indicators of failure. Each misstep, adjustment, or setback is an essential part of the journey, providing insights that ultimately make us stronger, wiser, and more capable.

One of the most liberating truths is that you don't have to be "ready" or have all the answers to begin. Often, it's through the process of taking imperfect action that clarity and confidence emerge. By starting where you are, with what you have, you open yourself up to possibilities that would remain hidden if you waited for the "perfect" moment. Progress over perfection means valuing the journey as much as the destination, celebrating each small win, and finding fulfillment in the act of moving forward.

Consider the artist who starts with a blank canvas. If they waited for the perfect inspiration or the assurance that every brushstroke would be flawless, they would never begin. But by picking up the brush and allowing themselves to explore, make mistakes, and experiment, they create something far more authentic and beautiful than any preconceived notion of perfection could ever achieve. The same is true for us. Our lives, our work, and our passions are the canvases on which we create, and it's through the willingness to take imperfect action that our greatest achievements come to life.

So, the next time you find yourself hesitating, waiting for everything to be "just right," remind yourself that progress is the real measure of success. Take that first step, no matter how small. Write the imperfect draft, start the conversation, make the bold decision. Every action you take brings you closer to your goals and reinforces the belief that you are capable, resilient, and enough just as you are. In choosing progress over perfection, you give yourself the freedom to grow, evolve, and ultimately, succeed in ways you never imagined possible.

Action Step: Embracing Imperfection in Your Journey

Now that we've explored the importance of letting go of perfection, it's time to put these insights into action. Here are practical steps to help you embrace imperfection, focus on progress, and move forward with confidence:

1. **Set "Imperfect" Goals:** Choose one area of your life—work, a personal project, or a relationship—where perfectionism has been holding you back. Set a goal that allows room for mistakes and learning. For example, instead of aiming to write a flawless report, commit to completing a draft within a set time, regardless of how polished it is. The goal is to take action, not to be perfect.

2. **Celebrate Small Wins:** At the end of each day, take a moment to reflect on your progress, no matter how small. Write down three things you accomplished, even if they seem insignificant. By acknowledging your efforts, you reinforce the habit of focusing on progress rather than perfection.

3. **Reframe Mistakes as Learning Opportunities:** The next time you make a mistake or face a setback, challenge yourself to view it as a valuable lesson rather than a failure. Ask yourself, "What can I learn from this experience?" or "How can this help me grow?" Over time,

this mindset shift will help you see imperfections as stepping stones on your journey.

4. **Take Action Before You're Ready:** Identify a task you've been putting off because it's not "perfect" yet, and commit to taking action within the next 24 hours. It could be sending that email, starting a new project, or sharing an idea with a colleague. Remember, clarity and confidence often come from doing, not from waiting for the perfect moment.

5. **Practice Self-Compassion:** Perfectionism is often rooted in self-criticism, so it's important to replace that inner critic with a more compassionate voice. When you catch yourself being overly harsh, pause and ask, "Would I speak to a friend this way?" Offer yourself the same kindness and understanding you would give to someone you care about.

6. **Embrace the "Good Enough" Mindset:** Choose one task this week that you'll intentionally complete to a "good enough" standard, rather than perfect. It might feel uncomfortable at first, but it will teach you that done is often better than perfect—and that the world won't fall apart if you let go of unrealistic expectations.

7. **Create a "Wins and Lessons" Journal:** Start a journal dedicated to tracking your daily wins and lessons learned from imperfections. This practice not only helps you focus on progress but also serves as a reminder that growth happens in the moments when we allow ourselves to be imperfect.

Ethan in Action: Releasing the Grip of Perfectionism

Ethan's opportunity to put this newfound mindset into action came sooner than he expected. He was preparing for an important presentation to his team—one that he had initially hoped would be flawless. As the deadline approached, Ethan found himself slipping back into old habits, revising his slides endlessly and agonizing over every word. The pressure to deliver a perfect presentation was overwhelming.

But this time, instead of allowing his perfectionism to control him, Ethan paused. He reminded himself of his commitment to embrace imperfection. He chose to stop obsessing over the details and focus on delivering a message that was authentic and meaningful, even if it wasn't perfect. He acknowledged that his imperfections didn't diminish the value of his work—they were what made it real and relatable.

On the day of the presentation, Ethan stood before his team and took a deep breath. Instead of reciting a rehearsed script, he spoke from the heart. He even shared a personal story about a recent failure and the lessons he learned from it. As he spoke, he felt a sense of relief wash over him. The pressure to be perfect melted away, replaced by a feeling of genuine connection with his audience.

After the presentation, one of his colleagues approached him with a smile. "I've never seen you so real before," she said. "It was inspiring to see you embrace your story, flaws and all." For the first time, Ethan realized that by letting go of perfection, he had allowed himself to be seen, not as a polished, untouchable figure but as a relatable human being who was still learning and growing.

This moment reinforced Ethan's belief that embracing imperfection was not a weakness but a source of strength. He began to see that the imperfections in his work and life were not barriers to success but stepping stones toward deeper authenticity and connection. By letting go of the need to be perfect, Ethan discovered the freedom to be himself—a lesson that would continue to shape his journey long after the presentation had ended.

Summary: Embracing Imperfection

In this chapter, we explored the profound impact of perfectionism on our lives, understanding how it often stems from a fear of failure and a need for external validation. This chapter shed light on how perfectionism can be paralyzing, keeping us trapped in a cycle of self-doubt and preventing us from taking the very steps necessary for growth and fulfillment. We saw how striving for flawlessness not only hinders our progress but also robs us of the joy that comes from engaging fully with life's experiences.

By embracing imperfection, we discovered the liberating truth that growth doesn't come from getting everything right the first time but from showing up, trying, failing, and trying again. We learned that our worth is not determined by how flawless we are but by our willingness to take action, take risks, and learn from our journey. Shifting our mindset from seeking perfection to valuing progress allows us to celebrate our achievements, however small, and to view mistakes as valuable lessons rather than evidence of inadequacy.

Key Takeaways

- **Perfectionism is Paralyzing**: Striving for perfection often leads to stagnation, fear of failure, and self-doubt. Letting go of this unrealistic standard allows us to take action, experiment, and grow through our imperfections.

- **Progress Over Perfection**: Shifting focus from flawless outcomes to consistent progress fosters resilience. Mistakes and setbacks are valuable learning experiences that help us improve and evolve.

- **Authenticity Fosters Connection**: Embracing imperfection enables more genuine connections with others. When we present our authentic, imperfect selves, we become more relatable, which strengthens our relationships and sense of belonging.

Conclusion: Embracing Imperfection as a Path to Growth

Embracing imperfection isn't about lowering your standards or settling for less; it's about giving yourself the freedom to grow, evolve, and pursue your goals without the burden of unrealistic expectations. When we let go of the need to be perfect, we create space for creativity, resilience, and meaningful connections in our lives. We learn to appreciate the beauty of our journey, with all its twists, turns, and messy moments, recognizing that it's in these very imperfections that our greatest strengths and insights are found.

As you continue on your path, remember that true success isn't about flawless execution; it's about having the courage to take imperfect action, to show up as you are, and to keep moving forward, one step at a time. Embrace your imperfections as signs of growth, celebrate your progress, and allow yourself the grace to be a work in progress. By doing so, you'll discover a more fulfilling, authentic version of success—one that's defined not by the absence of flaws but by the richness of your journey and the strength you gain along the way.

Conclusion

※

Embracing a New Definition of Success

Ethan stood by his office window, watching the city buzz with its usual sense of urgency. The skyline, once a symbol of relentless ambition and endless striving, now held a different meaning for him. He thought back to the person he was when this journey began—a man who measured his worth by his achievements, who believed that success was something to be chased, conquered, and displayed for all to see. But today, standing in the same place he had so often looked out from, he realized just how far he had come.

Ethan's journey wasn't a straight line. It was a winding path filled with detours, setbacks, and moments of doubt. There were times when he found himself slipping back into the familiar grip of hustle culture, believing that his value lay in how much he could produce or how hard he could push. But each time he stumbled, he took it as an opportunity to pause, reflect, and realign himself with the principles he had committed to—the principles of balance, mindfulness, and inner peace.

In learning to slow down, Ethan discovered that his drive and ambition didn't have to be sacrificed. In fact, they became more potent when tempered by moments of stillness. He began to understand that success wasn't about the titles, accolades, or recognition, but about how he felt at the end of each day—fulfilled, not just by what he had accomplished, but by how he had shown up for himself and others.

One pivotal moment stood out in his mind: a time when he faced a critical project deadline that threatened to pull him back into his old habits. The stress and pressure were intense, and the urge to revert to late nights and self-sacrifice was strong. But instead of giving in, Ethan chose to approach the challenge differently. He set boundaries, prioritized his well-being, and communicated openly with his team about his need for balance. It was a risk—one that could have been seen as a sign of weakness in the fast-paced world he inhabited. But to his surprise, it wasn't. His team responded with respect and support, and the project was completed not just successfully, but with a sense of ease and collaboration he had never experienced before.

This moment marked a turning point for Ethan, showing him that pursuing success and maintaining inner peace were not mutually exclusive. They could coexist, each enhancing the other in ways he had never imagined. He began to see that the very act of slowing down, of giving himself permission to breathe and be present, didn't diminish his drive—it amplified it. His creativity flourished, his relationships deepened, and his work took on a new level of meaning and impact.

Ethan's journey wasn't just about achieving a healthier work-life balance; it was about redefining what success meant to him. He realized that the moments of stillness he once saw as indulgent were, in fact, the spaces where his greatest insights emerged. It was in those pauses that he found clarity, renewed energy, and a deeper connection to his purpose. Success, he discovered, was not a finish line to be crossed but an ongoing journey that ebbed and flowed, much like life itself.

As he continued to grow in his career and personal life, Ethan found that his sense of peace became his greatest asset. It allowed him to navigate challenges with grace, approach setbacks with resilience, and engage with others from a place of authenticity and empathy. He no longer felt the need to constantly prove himself because he had already proven the most important thing of all—that he was worthy of success not because of what he did, but because of who he was.

Now, as he stood at that familiar window, Ethan felt a profound sense of gratitude. Not for the accolades or the achievements, but for the journey itself—the highs, the lows, the moments of doubt, and the moments of clarity. He had learned that success wasn't about reaching a destination but about embracing every step along the way, with all its imperfections and unpredictability.

As you close this book, let Ethan's journey serve as a reminder that your path, too, is uniquely yours to define. You don't have to choose between ambition and peace. You can have both, and in doing so, you'll find that your greatest achievements are not measured by how much you do, but by how deeply you live, how authentically you show up, and how courageously you embrace both the hustle and the stillness.

Ethan's story is an invitation to step off the treadmill of relentless striving and to walk a path that honors both your dreams and your well-being. It's a call to redefine success not as a race to be won but as a journey to be experienced fully, mindfully, and with a sense of inner calm. As you embark on your own journey, may you find, as Ethan did, that the real measure of success lies not in what you achieve but in how you feel, how you grow, and how you find peace within the pursuit.

As you reach the end of this journey, take a moment to reflect on the path you've traveled. Throughout this book, we've explored the cultural pressures that drive us to endlessly pursue achievement, the relentless hustle that promises fulfillment but often leaves us feeling empty, and the toll that this mindset takes on our well-being. We've also seen how, by embracing inner peace, resilience, and mindfulness, it's possible to pursue our ambitions in a way that honors both our dreams and our need for balance.

The truth is, our modern world often glorifies the hustle, encouraging us to measure our worth by our productivity, achievements, and external validation. But as we've discovered together, true success isn't defined by the hours we work, the titles we hold, or the accolades we accumulate. It's found in the quieter moments—the pauses, the reflections, and the choices we make that align with our deepest values.

This journey is not about giving up on your ambitions or settling for less. Instead, it's about redefining what it means to be truly successful. It's about recognizing that the most meaningful accomplishments are those that enrich our lives, foster genuine connections, and allow us to show up fully as ourselves. It's about understanding that the pursuit of success should not come at the cost of our well-being, relationships, or sense of self.

By cultivating inner peace, you've learned that you can navigate challenges with greater clarity and resilience. You've discovered that moments of stillness are not signs of laziness or weakness, but opportunities for growth, insight, and renewal. You've seen that success achieved at the expense of your mental, emotional, and physical health is not sustainable, and that a life driven solely by external markers of achievement will never be as fulfilling as one that is guided by a deeper sense of purpose and authenticity.

Just as Ethan discovered in his journey, embracing a more balanced approach doesn't mean abandoning your goals—it means pursuing them from a place of wholeness. When you integrate peace into your life, you create space for creativity, joy, and genuine connection. You give yourself permission to rest, to reflect, and to celebrate not just the big milestones, but the small, everyday victories that make life rich and meaningful.

The power of this approach lies in its ability to transform not only how you define success but how you experience it. When you pursue your dreams with a calm, centered mind, you're no longer driven by the fear of falling behind or the pressure to constantly do more. Instead, you're motivated by a desire to grow, to contribute, and to live a life that feels true to who you are. This shift in perspective allows you to move through life with greater intention, purpose, and fulfillment, turning every step of your journey into an opportunity for learning and self-discovery.

The path to finding balance between ambition and peace is not always easy. There will be moments when the pressure to conform to societal expectations will be overwhelming, and the temptation to fall back into old habits will be strong. But in those moments, remember that you have the tools, insights, and strength to choose differently. You have the power to redefine success on your own terms and to create a life that is not just about achieving, but about thriving.

As you move forward, let this book serve as a reminder that you don't have to choose between success and peace. You can have both. Allow yourself to embrace the ebb and flow of your journey, knowing that it's not about how fast you reach your destination, but about the quality of the experience along the way. Celebrate the moments of progress, learn from the setbacks, and cherish the times when you feel most connected to yourself and your purpose.

In the end, the greatest achievement you can reach is not the external validation that comes from others, but the sense of fulfillment that comes from living a life aligned with your values, aspirations, and true self. This is the quiet hustle—where you work diligently toward your goals while nurturing your inner peace, where you strive not out of fear or insecurity, but out of a genuine desire to grow and contribute.

So, as you close this book, ask yourself: *What would your life look like if you pursued your dreams with a sense of calm, clarity, and balance? What could you achieve if you allowed yourself to be both ambitious and at peace?*

The answer lies within you, waiting to be discovered. May you continue to find your own path, guided by the knowledge that true success is not a destination but a journey—one that is enriched by moments of stillness, reflection, and the quiet confidence that comes from living in harmony with who you truly are.

Thank you for allowing me to be part of your journey. As you move forward, I hope you carry with you the understanding that you are more than what you accomplish. You are worthy, not because of what you do, but because of who you are. And that, more than any accolade or achievement, is the ultimate measure of success.

Notes

[1] Deci, E. L., & Ryan, R. M. (2000). "The 'What' and 'Why' of Goal Pursuits: Human Needs and the Self-Determination of Behavior." Psychological Inquiry, 11(4), 227-268.

[2] Chou, H. T., & Edge, N. (2012). "They Are Happier and Having Better Lives Than I Am: The Impact of Using Facebook on Perceptions of Others' Lives." Cyberpsychology, Behavior, and Social Networking, 15(2), 117-121.

[3] Kasser, T., & Ryan, R. M. (1996). "Further Examining the American Dream: Differential Correlates of Intrinsic and Extrinsic Goals." Personality and Social Psychology Bulletin, 22(3), 280-287.

[4] Schwartz, S. J., Zamboanga, B. L., & Weisskirch, R. S. (2008). "Cultural stress and its relation to psychological functioning and academic engagement in Hispanic immigrant adolescents." *Journal of Youth and Adolescence*, 37(10), 1147–1159.

[5] Sapolsky, R. M. (2004). "Why Zebras Don't Get Ulcers: An Updated Guide to Stress, Stress-Related Diseases, and Coping." Holt Paperbacks.

[6] Wiking, M. (2016). "The Little Book of Hygge: Danish Secrets to Happy Living." William Morrow.

[7] Garcia, H., & Miralles, F. (2017). "Ikigai: The Japanese Secret to a Long and Happy Life." Penguin Books.

[8] World Health Organization. (2019). Burn-out an "occupational phenomenon": International Classification of Diseases. Retrieved from https://www.who.int/news/item/28-05-2019-burn-out-an-occupational-phenomenon-international-classification-of-diseases

[9] Gallup. (2020). Employee Burnout: Causes and Cures. Retrieved from https://www.gallup.com/workplace

[10] Catalin Cimpanu, "57% of Tech Workers Are Suffering From Job Burnout," BleepingComputer, June 25, 2018. Available at: https://www.bleepingcomputer.com/news/technology/57-percent-of-tech-workers-are-suffering-from-job-burnout/.

[11] Spring Health, "How to Prevent Employee Burnout at Your Organization," December 1, 2022. Accessed at: https://www.springhealth.com/blog/employee-burnout-management-prevention.

[12] The Independent: Katie Forster, "Japanese government tells people to stop overworking to combat death from excessive hours," January 18, 2017. Available at: The Independent.

[13] Ben Gilbert, "Elon Musk says people need to work around 80 hours per week to change the world," *Business Insider*, November 26, 2018. https://www.businessinsider.com/elon-musk-says-people-need-to-work-80-hours-per-week-2018-11.

[14] Gary Vaynerchuk, *Crush It!: Why Now Is the Time to Cash in on Your Passion* (New York: HarperCollins, 2009).

[15] Steers, M.-L. N., Wickham, R. E., & Acitelli, L. K., "Seeing Everyone Else's Highlight Reels: How Facebook Usage is Linked to Depressive Symptoms," *Journal of Social and Clinical Psychology*, 33(8), 701–731 (2014). https://doi.org/10.1521/jscp.2014.33.8.701

[16] World Health Organization, *Burn-out an "Occupational Phenomenon": International Classification of Diseases*, 2019. https://www.who.int/mental_health/evidence/burn-out/en/

[17] World Health Organization, "Long Working Hours and Their Impact on Health," WHO Report, 2021, https://www.who.int/publications/i/item/9789240027043.

[18] Sapolsky, R. M. (2004). *Why Zebras Don't Get Ulcers: The Acclaimed Guide to Stress, Stress-Related Diseases, and Coping*. Holt Paperbacks.

[19] Melamed, Samuel, et al. "Burnout and Risk of Cardiovascular Disease: Evidence, Possible Causal Paths, and Promising Research Directions," Journal of Occupational Health Psychology 11, no. 3 (2006): 299-312.

[20] Gino, Francesca, and Michael Norton, "Why We're So Lonely—and How to Overcome It," Harvard Business Review, March 2018, https://hbr.org/2018/03/why-were-so-lonely-and-how-to-overcome-it.

[21] John T. Cacioppo and Louise C. Hawkley, "Social Isolation and Health, with an Emphasis on Underlying Mechanisms," *Perspectives in Biology and Medicine* 46, no. 3 (2003): S39-S52. https://doi.org/10.1353/pbm.2003.0063.

[22] John Pencavel, "The Productivity of Working Hours," *The Economic Journal* 125, no. 589 (2014): 2052-2076. https://doi.org/10.1111/ecoj.12166.

[23] Lippelt, D. P., Hommel, B., & Colzato, L. S. (2014). *Focused Attention, Open Monitoring and Loving Kindness Meditation: Effects on Attention, Conflict Monitoring, and Creativity – A Review. Frontiers in Psychology, 5*, 1083. https://doi.org/10.3389/fpsyg.2014.01083

[24] *Emmons, R. A., & McCullough, M. E. (2003). "Counting Blessings Versus Burdens: An Experimental Investigation of Gratitude and Subjective Well-Being in Daily Life."* Journal of Personality and Social Psychology, 84(2), 377–389.

Clance, P. R., & Imes, S. A. (1978). The impostor phenomenon in high achieving women: Dynamics and therapeutic intervention. *Psychotherapy: Theory, Research & Practice*, 15(3), 241–247.[25]

[26] Obama, M. (2018). *Becoming*. Crown Publishing Group.

[27] Gross, T. (2016). Tom Hanks on 'Fresh Air' [Interview]. *NPR*. https://www.npr.org

[28] "Meditation Has Power In Sports," *Sports Psychology Today*, accessed October 2, 2024, https://www.sportpsychologytoday.com.

[29] "How Top CEOs Reduce Stress in the Workplace," *Ross & Ross International*, accessed October 2, 2024, https://www.rossross.com/blog/how-top-ceos-reduce-stress-in-the-workplace.

[30] Elizabeth Gilbert, "On Fear and Creativity," *Conferences for Women*, accessed October 2, 2024, https://www.conferencesforwomen.org/elizabeth-gilbert-on-fear-and-creativity/.

[31] "50 Famous People Who Meditate," *MeditationWise*, accessed October 2, 2024, www.meditationwise.com.

[32] "How to Remain Calm Like Buffett in Turbulent Times," *GuruFocus*, accessed October 2, 2024, https://www.gurufocus.com.

[33] "Don't Flip Your Lid: The Intersection of Mindfulness and Neuroscience," *IMCW*, accessed October 2, 2024, https://imcw.org/blogs/dont-flip-your-lid-the-intersection-of-mindfulness-and-neuroscience/.

[34] Walter Isaacson, *Steve Jobs* (New York: Simon & Schuster, 2011).

[35] "How JK Rowling Turned Rejection Into Success," *Business Insider*, accessed October 2, 2024, https://www.businessinsider.com/jk-rowling-rejection-success.

[36] Brown, K.W., & Ryan, R.M., "The Benefits of Being Present: Mindfulness and Its Role in Psychological Well-Being," *Journal of Personality and Social Psychology*, 84(4), 822–848.

[37] Robert Root-Bernstein and Michele Root-Bernstein, *Einstein on Creative Thinking: Music and the Intuitive Art of Scientific Imagination*, *Psychology Today*, accessed October 2, 2024, https://www.psychologytoday.com.

[38] Baird, B., Smallwood, J., Mrazek, M. D., et al. "Inspired by Distraction: Mind Wandering Facilitates Creative Incubation," *Psychological Science*, 23(10), 1117–1122.

[39] "The Leadership Legacy of Howard Schultz: Lessons in Innovation, Community, and Social Responsibility," *Untitled Leader*, accessed October 2, 2024, https://www.untitledleader.com.

[40] "Patagonia Founder Gives Away the $3bn Company to Environmental Causes," *The Independent*, accessed October 2, 2024, https://www.independent.co.uk.

[41] Rebecca Muller Feintuch, "The One Question Oprah Wants You to Ask Yourself at Work," *Thrive Global*, accessed October 2, 2024.

[42] Derek Beres, "'Mindful' People Are Better Goal-Setters According to New Research," *Big Think*, accessed October 2, 2024, https://bigthink.com.

[43] "Finding Focus and Owning Your Attention," *Brené Brown*, accessed October 2, 2024, https://brenebrown.com.

[44] "Mindfulness in the Workplace: Does It Really Work?" *APA*, accessed October 2, 2024. https://www.apa.org.

[45] Neff, K. D. (2011). *Self-compassion: The proven power of being kind to yourself*. William Morrow.

[46] Florida Atlantic University. (2020, September 9). Mindfulness with paced breathing and lowering blood pressure. *ScienceDaily*. Retrieved October 19, 2024, from https://www.sciencedaily.com/releases/2020/09/200909100214.htm

[47] American Psychological Association. (2018). *Stress effects on the body*. Retrieved from https://www.apa.org/topics/stress/body

[48] Harvard Medical School. (2007). *Sleep and mental health*. Harvard Health Publishing. Retrieved from https://www.health.harvard.edu/newsletter_article/sleep-and-mental-health

[49] American Psychological Association. (2019). Give yourself a break: The power of taking time off. *Monitor on Psychology, 50*(1). https://www.apa.org/monitor/2019/01/break

[50] Cirillo, F. (2006). *The Pomodoro Technique*. Pomodoro Technique.

[51] Johnson, Spencer. *Who Moved My Cheese?* Putnam Adult, 1998.

[52] Brown, Brené. *The Gifts of Imperfection: Let Go of Who You Think You're Supposed to Be and Embrace Who You Are*. Hazelden Publishing, 2010.

[53] Emmons, Robert A. *Gratitude Works!: A 21-Day Program for Creating Emotional Prosperity*. Jossey-Bass, 2013.

[54] Emmons, Robert A., and Michael E. McCullough. "Counting Blessings Versus Burdens: An Experimental Investigation of Gratitude and Subjective Well-Being in Daily Life." *Journal of Personality and Social Psychology*, vol. 84, no. 2, 2003, pp. 377-389.

[55] Clear, James. *Atomic Habits: An Easy & Proven Way to Build Good Habits & Break Bad Ones*. Avery, 2018.

Index

A Letter to You, The Reader

Dear Reader,

Thank you from the bottom of my heart for taking the time to read The Quiet Hustle: Balancing Stress with Stillness. I hope that through these pages, you've found insights and practices that resonate with your journey toward balance and inner peace. Life can be demanding, and it's easy to get swept away in the hustle, but my hope is that you've discovered ways to reclaim your calm and embrace a more sustainable path to success.

While these ideas and practices have been profoundly meaningful for me, I want to be transparent—I am not a psychologist or psychiatrist. I'm simply someone who has navigated the pressures of life and found peace in stillness. The tools and perspectives I've shared are not a replacement for professional mental health care, but rather a complement to it. If you ever feel overwhelmed or like you're struggling with your mental health, I encourage you to seek guidance from a licensed professional who can provide the support and care you deserve.

If you or someone you know is in need of help, here are a few resources that may be helpful:

- National Suicide Prevention Lifeline: 1-800-273-TALK (1-800-273-8255)

- Substance Abuse and Mental Health Services Administration (SAMHSA): 1-800-662-HELP (1-800-662-4357)

- Crisis Text Line: Text HOME to 741741

- National Alliance on Mental Illness (NAMI) Helpline: 1-800-950-NAMI (1-800-950-6264)

Remember, you are never alone on this journey. Seeking support is a sign of strength, not weakness.

Thank you once again for allowing me to share my story with you. I am grateful for your time and attention, and I wish you continued success, peace, and fulfillment as you move forward in life.

With deepest gratitude,
Wes

Special Thanks

As I bring The Quiet Hustle to a close, I want to take a moment to extend my deepest gratitude to those who have supported me along this journey. Writing this book has been a deeply personal endeavor, and I couldn't have done it without the encouragement and contributions of many wonderful people.

To my wife, Amanda, your unwavering love and belief in me are the foundation of everything I do. Thank you for your patience, your insight, and for always reminding me to find balance in my own life.

To my family and friends, your constant support and willingness to listen to my ideas have meant more to me than I can express. Your feedback, whether large or small, helped shape this book into what it is today.

A special thank you to my teachers and mentors for guiding me through my education, career, and personal growth. Your wisdom and perspective have been invaluable, and your influence is felt throughout these pages.

To my colleagues and peers who shared their experiences and insights, thank you for inspiring me to push deeper into understanding the importance of stillness and resilience in our busy world.

And finally, thank you to every reader who has picked up this book. Your time, attention, and openness to exploring new perspectives are greatly appreciated. It is my sincere hope that The Quiet Hustle helps you find calm amidst the chaos and peace in your own personal and professional life.

Thank you from the bottom of my heart!

About The Author

Wes Bozarth, author of *The Quiet Hustle: Balancing Stress with Stillness*, was inspired by his personal journey of finding calm amidst the pressures of modern life. With over a decade of professional experience in engineering and continuous improvement, Wes combines practical advice with deep mindfulness practices such as meditation and affirmations. His mission is to help readers find stillness in the stress and build a purposeful life. Wes holds advanced degrees in science from Western Kentucky University. He lives with his wife in Owensboro, Kentucky, where he strives to cultivate a life of balance, purpose, and mindfulness each day.

Contact The Author

I'd love to hear from you! Whether you have thoughts about the book, questions, or stories you'd like to share, feel free to reach out to me at wbozarth@live.com. While I read every message, please understand that it may take some time for me to respond, and I may not be able to respond to all. Thank you for your support and for being a part of this journey.